DAVID &
CHARLES
BRITAIN

THE
LAKE DIST

D1491527

£1-00.

Daphne Wyatt

Other titles in this series:
THE YORKSHIRE DALES
Geoffrey Wright

SNOWDONIA
William Condry

THE PEMBROKESHIRE COAST NATIONAL PARK
Dillwyn Miles

THE
LAKE DISTRICT

Michael Dunn

David & Charles
Newton Abbot   London   North Pomfret (Vt)

(title page)
The rounded slopes of the north-western fells, composed of Skiddaw Slates, from the track to Hause Gate, between Catbells and Maiden Moor. Scar Crags and the unusually knobbly summit of Causey Pike are on the left

British Library Cataloguing in Publication Data

Dunn, Michael, 1948-
    The Lake District.———(David & Charles
    Britain).
    1. Lake District (England)———Description
    and travel———Guide-books
    I. Title
    914.27'804858   DA670.L1

ISBN 0–7153–8997–1

Phototypeset by ABM Typographics, Hull
Printed in Great Britain
by Butler & Tanner Limited, Frome and London
for David & Charles Publishers plc
Brunel House   Newton Abbot   Devon

Published in the United States of America
by David & Charles Inc
North Pomfret   Vermont 05053   USA

CONTENTS

INTRODUCTION:
MY NATIONAL PARK

My first introduction to the Lake District, more than twenty years ago, left impressions which must be all too familiar to summer visitors. Mist and rain drifted over fell and dale, reputedly spectacular views were near at hand but infuriatingly were glimpsed only imperfectly, promising walks were curtailed and the wet slate towns of Keswick and Ambleside became well known.

But the special attractions of the district had clearly ensnared me, for later in the 1960s I was back, much more regularly now, based at a cottage in the far western fells and exploring the largely unfrequented country between Ennerdale and Wasdale. The list of unlikely ascents included Lank Rigg and Grike, Herdus and Haycock – this one, together with Pillar, conquered on a raw December day in driving snow yet providing a marvellously exhilarating walk. These were the days, too, of hound trails and Cumberland hotpot on New Year's Day, of Egremont crab fair in the autumn, and of leisurely evenings – and early mornings – in Ennerdale Bridge and Calder Bridge.

This was also the time of my first acquaintance with Blencathra, the mountain that was to become my personal favourite. First impressions

Buttermere village and lake, with the slopes of High Stile beyond Burtness Wood

An early morning view of the head of Wastwater, with Yewbarrow to the left, the slopes of Lingmell and Scafell Pike to the right, and the summit of Great Gable still wreathed in mist were once again deceptive: we missed the path to Scales Tarn and later found ourselves, ill-equipped, kicking steps in the snow up a steep gully onto Sharp Edge. The ascent, thankfully, was abandoned but the magic of the mountain had struck a chord and I was to return on countless occasions, becoming familiar not only with Sharp Edge and Foule Crag but also with Hall's Fell and Doddick Fell and, at a lower level, Gategill and the excellent approach from Mungrisdale, that most delectable of Cumbrian hamlets.

Still more surprises were in store in the 1980s when, with a young family in tow, I discovered the lower fells. High Rigg is an outstanding example; a mere pimple to peak-baggers, it offers a wonderfully varied walk with grassy paths and little rocky turrets, and has as fine a view as many more exalted fells, with Blencathra and Skiddaw, the craggy north-western outliers of the Helvellyn range and the attractively grouped north-western fells all displayed to advantage.

Many more facets of lower-level Lakeland took on greater significance, too, and increasingly I became fascinated by the rich archaeological and historical heritage of the area. I explored stone circles and standing stones, revelling in the extraordinary air of mystery surrounding Swinside and Moor Divock. I puzzled over the routes of Roman roads and confessed bafflement at the supposed 'thing-mount' in Little Langdale. I explored pele towers, castles, statesman farmhouses and above all the surviving medieval fragments of the monks' short-lived supremacy. And all the time the Lake District remained tantalisingly capable of new surprises and new delights. No one will ever be able to say they know it completely.

My early introduction to the western Lake District was invaluable. More than anything else it impressed on me the scope for escape from the inevitably crowded honeypots to quieter spots where spectacular surroundings, the natural history of the area or more intimate facets of the landscape could be enjoyed more peacefully and at leisure. Wonderful walks, for example in Back o' Skidda' country, meeting only one other walker in a whole day; visits to historical or industrial monuments such as the Roman forts, the mills at Caldbeck or the abbey ruins or dale chapels; nature strolls in Johnny Wood or on Claife Heights or Whitbarrow Scar; all these and more spring to memory as special days spent far from the madding crowd.

The result is that although in times of exile from the Lake District my mind's eye may well conjure up classic images such as that of early morning Wasdale, with the shimmering but still vaguely threatening expanse of Wastwater a magical foreground for the misty ring of outstanding mountains at its head, or the deeply eroded southern face of Blencathra, with the irresistible challenges of its rocky ridges and deeply riven gullies, it also ranges widely over a remarkable diversity of experiences freely available to Lakeland visitors. Days on Hallin Fell or Mellbreak can provide as much pleasure as more demanding expeditions around the head of Eskdale or on the Helvellyn edges; the spinning galleries of Hartsop and the pele towers of the Lake District fringes rival more celebrated venues such as Lowther Castle, Hill Top Farm or Dove Cottage. And, as succeeding chapters of this book make clear, even this menu of widely varying attractions does scant justice to the outstanding qualities of the Lake District, truly the jewel in England's crown.

1
LAKE DISTRICT PANORAMA

The perfect location, the exact spot from which to take in the essence of the Lake District: many will have an idea for such a viewpoint. For some it will be Orrest Head above Windermere, with the Langdale Pikes prominent in the westerly view. Others will quote Skiddaw Little Man, that outstanding belvedere for the high fells beyond Derwentwater; still others will opt for the prospect of the tremendous group of mountains at Wasdale Head, or perhaps Helvellyn and Striding Edge from the slopes of Place Fell, across the head of Ullswater and the Patterdale valley.

Sadly, none of these will do. Neither, despite its quite superb all-round panorama, will the viewpoint I have chosen to illustrate some of the distinctive features of the Lake District. For the simple truth is that no one viewpoint can represent the greatest single asset of the region, namely the immense variety of scenery both between and within the dales. Nevertheless, we have to begin somewhere, and though my choice of starting point, Dale Head in the north-western fells, may surprise some, the quality of the prospect from its splendid cairn will surely enchant many more. The best approach is from Newlands, either up the dale or along one of the flanking ridges, but let us assume that we have taken the shorter and easier path from Honister, arriving at the top of Dale Head with time to spare. There is plenty to see, for this is one of the most revealing viewpoints in the Lake District, as well as one of the most exciting.

Map 1   The Lake District (over 600m shaded)

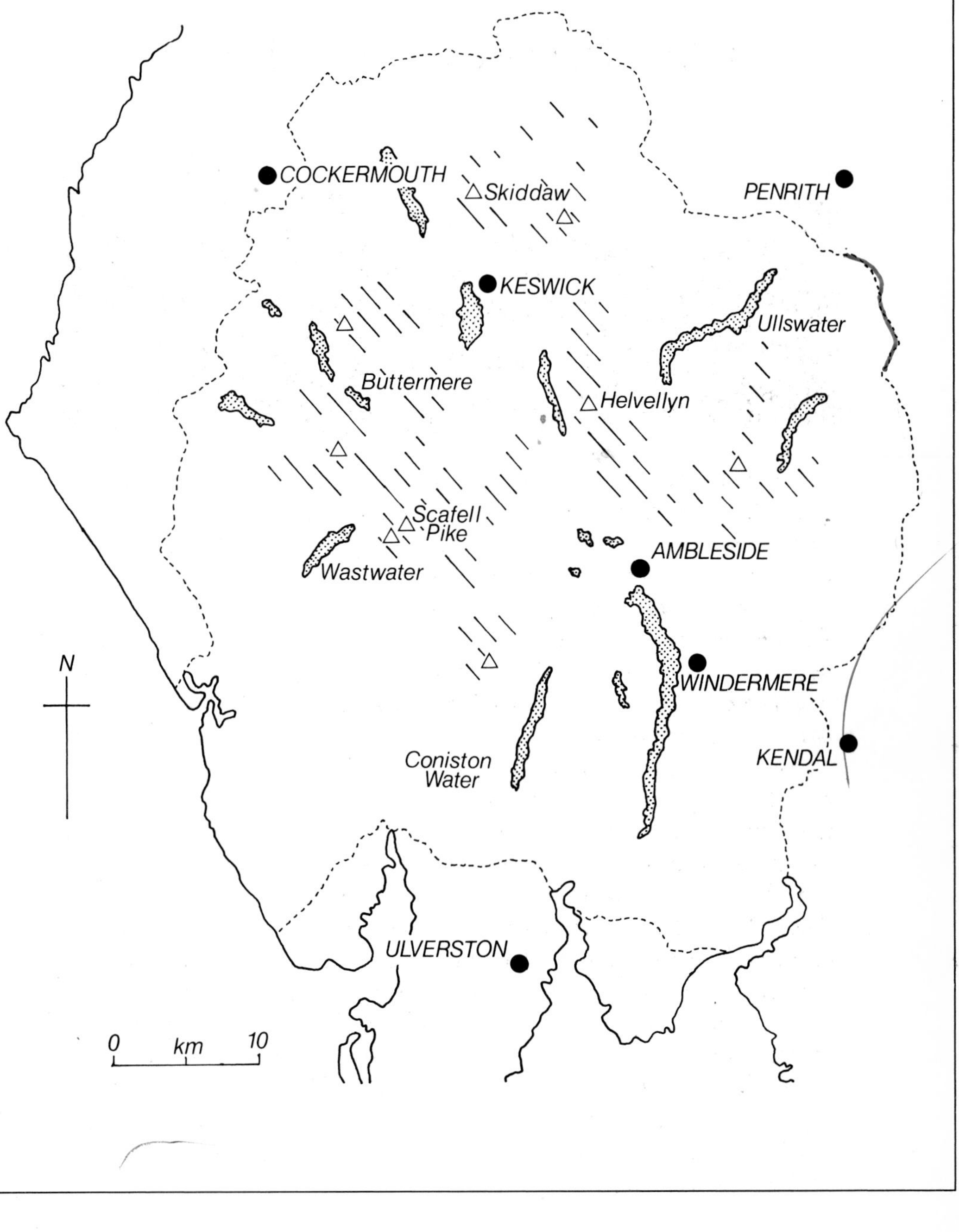

COCKERMOUTH

△Skiddaw

PENRITH

KESWICK

Ullswater

△

Buttermere

△Helvellyn

Scafell
Pike
△
△

Wastwater

△

△

AMBLESIDE

△

WINDERMERE

KENDAL

N

Coniston
Water

ULVERSTON

0   km   10

The highest point is marked by a shapely and attractive cairn and is superbly situated at the head of the Newlands valley, with panoramic views of the main mountain groups. The spectacular downfall into Newlands leads the eye along the mine road threading its way down the dale (a hint of the area's remarkable industrial past, with mines below Scope End, at Castle Nook and on the higher slopes of Dale Head itself) past the little wooded hill of Swinside to the tremendous bulk of Skiddaw, flanked by buttressing fells such as Ullock Pike and Lonscale Fell. These gently rounded fells are characteristic of Skiddaw Slate country, though the east side of Newlands, with Eel Crags dropping abruptly below the summit of High Spy, serves as a pertinent reminder that there are also outbreaks of naked rock in these apparently gentle northern fells. Bassenthwaite Lake is glimpsed to the left of Skiddaw, while to the right is Carrock Fell, its summit crowned by an Iron Age hillfort. The south face of Blencathra, silhouetted above Eel Crags, is a further indication that this is a landscape of infinite variety: the broad flanks of the fell contrast starkly with the dramatically narrow central ridges and deep gullies, and above it all there is a fine summit perched at the edge of the abyss.

To the east, beyond the well-wooded glacial trench of Borrowdale (it's a pity that so little of this delectable and varied dale can be seen), the long serrated skyline of the Helvellyn massif can be seen in its entirety, with half a dozen northerly summits culminating in the celebrated and immensely popular top of Helvellyn itself, directly to the east of Dale Head. Between Helvellyn and Fairfield the highest point of the Lake District's most easterly ridge, High Street, can just be glimpsed. Though far from the centre of things this is a fine mountain – and an historic one, too, with a Roman road travelling along its crest – and after being neglected for decades by fellwalkers it has now come into its own, as witness the often congested car park at Mardale Head. The sight of the col at Greenup Edge recalls another ancient route, that of the medieval packhorse trail from Borrowdale to Grasmere.

The Dale Head panorama is just as spectacular to the south, with the distant tops of the Langdale Pikes, those most instantly recognisable of the Lakeland fells, to the left of a remarkable skyline hinting at the majesty of the highest land in Britain – the shapely Bowfell, Esk Pike, the tremendous northern crags of Great End and, highest of all, Scafell Pike and Scafell. Just to the right the great north face of Great Gable is particularly prominent. The path from Honister to Great Gable can clearly be seen, together with Moses' Trod, the smugglers' route to Wasdale, later reused by quarrymen carrying Honister slate to the coast

The top of Dale Head, with its magnificent summit cairn. The view to the east includes Blencathra (extreme left) and the long ridge of the Helvellyn range (see also colour photograph page 136)

on rough sledges. Still further right, just beyond the distinctive notch of the Black Sail Pass (used by another ancient route), Pillar and the High Stile range define the position of the unseen Ennerdale, possibly the least visited of all the dales. Buttermere, commonly regarded as the prettiest dale, lies just to the left of Robinson, and finally, somewhat nearer at hand, Grasmoor and its neighbours occupy the north-western quadrant, immediately left of that splendid view along the Newlands valley.

The all-round panorama is stupendous, then, but there is no point in pretending that we have so far done more than scratch the surface in describing the landscape of the Lake District. We have hinted at the industrial history of the area – yet mining was only one of a number of basic industries which once flourished. Even more superficial has been the reference to man's earlier influence on the landscape, not just in prehistory – the Iron Age fort on Carrock Fell is by no means the most spectacular of the many survivals – but also in understanding more recent effects, from Norse settlement to monastic colonisation and later agricultural changes. Most important of all, we have seen little of the natural history of the area, from the formation of the landscape to the fauna and flora which it now supports.

Perhaps the first lesson to learn is that the highest viewpoint is not necessarily the best. Dale Head, for all its merits, cannot boast any really satisfying views of the one cohesive element in this area of diversity, namely the lakes themselves. And it is true that the best views of the lakes are generally obtained at mid-height – above the valley floor, in order to introduce scale into the scene, but below the mountain summits, where the true perspective can be lost amid a welter of distant and sometimes uncertain images.

Amongst many lower level views which are especially memorable one of the best is the sight of the Langdale Pikes and the central backbone of the Lake District from Sweden Bridge Lane above Ambleside, with upland pastures strewn with boulders and little rock outcrops making an effective foreground, and the rare jewel of Rydal Water in the middle distance. On a grander scale the prospect of the upper Buttermere valley from the banks of Sourmilk Gill, at the entrance to Bleaberry Comb and halfway up Red Pike, is just as satisfying. Buttermere itself, a splash of dark blue in the surprisingly green lakeside meadows (thick with buttercups in spring) is backed by the massif of Robinson and, to the right of the road picking its way up Gatesgarthdale to the Honister Pass, the jutting spine of Fleetwith Pike, by no means the highest of Lakeland's mountains but from this angle one of the very best.

Undoubtedly the main attraction for many, typified by the view of Buttermere and Fleetwith Pike, is the interplay of fellside and water – the sight of the lakes in their mountain setting. Nowhere is this better illustrated than in the prospect from the top of Hallin Fell, small in stature and easily conquered but not easily forgotten. The view from the rocky summit, with its spectacularly solid cairn, is remarkable both to the north, where the sylvan lower reaches of Ullswater are unfolded, and to the west and south-west, where the middle section of this splendidly scenic lake is displayed in front of Helvellyn and its acolytes.

Splendid though these examples of the special qualities inherent in the intermingling of lake and fell are, they by no means exhaust the variety which is the hallmark of the area. Neither do they do justice to the smaller, more intimate features of the landscape which are so important in explaining the attractions of the Lake District. These subtler features range from the tarns, often merely glimpsed in shady hollows, to the major crags such as Dow Crag and, thrusting up startlingly in St John's Vale, the Castle Rock of Triermain; from the passes, many of them high and remote, to the more urban delights of settlements such as Troutbeck and Hawkshead; and from that most humble but essential of man's early contributions to the landscape, the packhorse bridge, to the industrial heritage of spinning galleries and bobbin mills, and indeed iron smelting sites and lead and copper mines. There is, too, the mystical – the stone circles and burial mounds, for instance – and the religious, with Viking crosses and medieval monasteries.

The tarns need no introduction. The most indolent of tourists can see a number of them to advantage without stirring far on foot: Blea Tarn, for example, perched between the two Langdales and with a stupendous backdrop of the Langdale Pikes, or Tarn Hows, this one man-made but nevertheless deservedly popular. The best of them need a little more effort, however. There is no need to go to the lengths of scaling Scafell to see Foxes Tarn, for this is an insignificant little pool (so too is Broadcrag Tarn, the highest tarn of all, away from the tourist routes on Scafell Pike). It *is* worth persevering as far as the corrie basins, or coves, which nestle below the summit plateaux of many of the main fells. Angle Tarn, below the black, brooding crags of Bowfell, is a well-known example on a very well used path into the fells; Stickle Tarn above Great Langdale, with its tremendous back wall leading up to Pavey Ark, is amongst the most visited; and for the sheer magnificence of the encircling scenery even this one is surpassed by Goat's Water, a classic mountain tarn in a rock-strewn basin below the tremendous cliffs of Dow Crag. Not all the Lake District's tarns are so spectacular: quite a number, such as Scoat Tarn in the western fells and the much-photographed Watendlath Tarn, sit in comparatively wide basins, but nevertheless they add their distinctive and welcome contribution to the overall scene.

Mention has already been made of the craggy northern buttresses of Bowfell and the astonishing rock wall of Dow Crag, and this is no coincidence; many of the outstanding crags in the Lake District rise dramatically and picturesquely above upland waters. This is not universally the case, however. Scafell Crag rises precipitously above the stony wastes of Hollow Stones, and walkers will often see rock climbers at work on the crag. The famous scree shoot of Lord's Rake is here, between the crag and Shamrock Buttress, and though this is steep and treacherously difficult in places, it is at least accessible to ordinary mortals. Pillar Rock obeys the same principles as Scafell Crag, rising sheer from the scree-laden slopes of Ennerdale and being best viewed from a distance – in this case preferably from Robinson's Cairn, a staging post on what is incomparably the best way to the summit of Pillar, blessed with a superb view of the spectacular complexities of the Rock.

The route from Wasdale to Pillar via Robinson's Cairn makes first for the Black Sail Pass, one of the finest passes in the Lake District, separating the deep U-shaped glaciated bowl of Mosedale from the desolate wastes of upper Ennerdale – one of the remotest parts of the National Park. As with many of the district's other passes it is not only attractive but also of considerable antiquity as a through route connecting adjacent dales. Its name, too, is specially evocative – but this applies to a number of others, such as Sticks Pass in the Helvellyn range, at its busiest when lead from the Greenside mine above Glenridding was carted westwards to the smelter at Brigham near Keswick, and named after the stakes driven into the ground to define the route when the track itself, rising to almost 750m (2,450ft) at the pass, was obscured by snow.

The dales of the eastern Lake District are almost without exception connected by these ancient routes. From Mardale Head, above the reservoir of Haweswater, two such routes, both used by packhorses in medieval times, ascend the flanking slopes of Harter Fell. To the left, the way to Longsleddale lies over the Gatescarth Pass; to the right, a wonderfully scenic route runs up to the delightful tarn of Small Water, where there are some curious low shelters next to the path, before climbing to the sharply defined rocky defile of the Nan Bield Pass and dropping down, just as steeply and again over rough ground, to the head of the Kentmere valley and eventually the hamlet of Kentmere itself. Pack trains unbowed by the severity of the Nan Bield ascent could then traverse the Garburn Pass, following a route clearly defined by an outcrop of the relatively soft Coniston Limestone, on their way to Troutbeck and the heart of the Lake District. The wonder of this route, outstanding by any standards, is that it can be followed at leisure by walkers nowadays.

The Garburn Road leads down into the village of Troutbeck, one of the truly exceptional villages of the region, with a scatter of 'statesman' farmhouses dating from the seventeenth century grouped around a series of wells along the valley side, and an attractive church away from the village in the Trout Beck valley. The National Trust farmhouse at Town End packs them in, but any number are worth seeing, though very few still function as the centre of working farms. Hartsop, near the head of the Patterdale valley, is equally attractive but equally invaded by second-home owners to the detriment of the full-time life of the village.

Hartsop boasts a number of excellent examples of a style of architecture characteristic of the rural Lake District – the external spinning gallery in which the yarn for much of the district's woollen industry was spun. The best surviving examples are those at Mireside and Thorn House, though there are others which can be seen in a stroll through the hamlet. Examples elsewhere include those at Yew Tree Farm near Coniston and Hodge Hill and Pool Bank, both on Cartmel Fell. Spinning galleries were perhaps the least industrialised forms of Lake District industry; the woollen mills at locations such as Millbeck, near Keswick, and Caldbeck – the forlorn hulk of the mill is still hauntingly present here – hint at the perhaps inevitable increase in concentration of an activity which had begun as a true cottage industry.

Woollens were by no means the staple industry of the Lake District, however, despite the burgeoning presence of sheep from early medieval times onwards. Two factors were crucial to the importance of the area in early medieval times: mineral wealth and the availability of water

The spinning gallery at Thorn House, Hartsop, a classic example of this very localised architectural tradition

power. The mineral wealth of the district was perceived to be so important that Daniel Hochstetter and his teams of German miners were imported – not without some local resentment – to exploit the resources of the mines in the Newlands valley and, somewhat later, the copper mines which brought considerable prosperity to the village of Coniston. Mining was of significant economic importance at several other centres, too, including Threlkeld, where the Gategill lead mine brought brief but substantial prosperity, and Glenridding, a village which to all intents and purposes owes its existence to the Greenside lead mine, tremendously successful at first but later a curse rather than a blessing on the valley when the Keppelcove reservoir burst its banks and unleashed a torrent on the unsuspecting village.

Nowadays, though the mines of the Lake District are disused, they are of considerable historical and visual interest, and not only geologists are attracted to sites such as Coppermines Valley at Coniston, the Carrock Mine in the upper Caldew valley in the depths of Skiddaw Forest and the Dale Head mine at the head of the Newlands valley – the latter two in particular still combed by interested amateurs searching for specimens. And whilst the mines of the Lake District are no more, slate quarrying, which can trace its history as an organised industry at least as far back as 1643, when the Honister quarries were already in production, still continues at a number of locations in and around the National Park, and the granite quarries at Shap are still very much in production.

A brief survey of the industrial past of the Lake District, especially one concentrating on its visible survivals, must also include the woodland industries of the southern part of the district, such as the bobbin mills at Low Stott Park and Spark Bridge, the early iron smelting sites such as that at Cunsey and the later, more sophisticated sites at Backbarrow and elsewhere. Above all, perhaps, it should draw the visitor's attention to the earlier industrial phase largely brought about through the initiative and enterprise of the monks. Furness Abbey in particular was quick to exploit the resources placed at its disposal, establishing primitive open hearths (bloomeries), fed with charcoal produced from the abundant woodlands in its High Furness estates, to smelt iron ore at, for instance, Cinder Hill above Newby Bridge. The evocatively named Smithymire Island at the confluence of the Langstrath Beck and Greenup Gill was another early bloomery site.

The monks were also assiduous in cultivating the fellsides, populating them thickly with sheep. A surviving thirteenth-century charter explains the significance of a strange ditch and bank which

Matty Benn's Bridge, the historic but now disused and overgrown packhorse bridge over the River Calder. Its construction is attributed to the monks of Calder Abbey, who used it in driving their flocks to the vast sheepwalks on the fells between Wasdale and Ennerdale

traverses Great Moss in upper Eskdale: this was the boundary bank of the monks' estate, carefully constructed to keep the sheep in whilst allowing the deer to get out. Even more tangible evidence of the monks' presence is provided by some of the surviving packhorse bridges, a specially attractive landscape element in which the Lake District is peculiarly rich. The sheep pasturing in Great Moss, for example, were driven there over a splendid single-arched packhorse bridge spanning the Lingcove Beck just above its confluence with the River Esk. Though the present bridge is a classic example it is, in fact, a recent replacement, its predecessor having been seriously damaged by floods. Just below the bridge is the Throstle Garth sheepfold, in continuous use since it was first constructed in medieval times by the Furness monks.

Matty Benn's Bridge, deep in the Calder valley in the western Lake District, is another fine example of a packhorse bridge – this time authentically ancient – which owes its origin to a monastic foundation. The monks of Calder Abbey are credited with its construction; indeed its alternative name is Monks' Bridge. Not all the district's packhorse bridges are explained in this way, however. In Wasdale, Row Head Bridge (highly photogenic with the Mosedale Beck rippling beneath and Kirk Fell rising steeply in the background) was originally an integral part of the main route down the dale from Wasdale Head; the present road avoiding the bridge is a modern realignment. Still other bridges served only very local requirements: Folly Bridge in Ennerdale and Willy Goodwaller Bridge in Easedale were used only in driving sheep between adjacent pastures, whilst others which are picturesque but unrelated to packhorse or even sheep movement include the delightful Slater Bridge in Little Langdale, a slate slab bridge allowing quarrymen from the Langdales to get to work in the Wetherlam quarries. Just as picturesque but even less associated with ancient trading routes are the various sets of stepping stones, for instance Stythwaite Steps in Far Easedale and those across the Esk near Boot and the Duddon near Seathwaite.

Finally, in this whirlwind tour of the area's manifold attractions we turn to the mystical, and in many cases the unexplained. The most celebrated of these phenomena is the stone circle, often massive in scale and therefore awesome in execution, but of deeply uncertain purpose. Castlerigg, to the east of Keswick, is the most accessible and best known of the district's stone circles, though there are others such as The Cockpit on Moor Divock above Ullswater, and the best is probably the Swinside stone circle in the far south-west, a particularly impressive sight in the otherwise empty vastness of the grassy Black Combe fells. Burial mounds are a different kettle of fish: in some areas they are thick on the ground – 1,200 have been identified in the immediate vicinity of Devoke Water, south of Eskdale, for example – yet in others they are strangely absent. Most are round barrows, characteristic of the Bronze Age, though there are exceptions such as the Neolithic cairn of Sampson's Bratful, a long barrow on Stockdale Moor, in the remote and almost unvisited upland between Ennerdale and Wasdale.

The Norse settlement of the dales, though more recent, is scarcely any easier to comprehend. The surviving artefacts are too few and too disparate to enable us to build a complete picture, though some of them represent immensely powerful images. The Viking cross in the church-yard at Gosforth, on the coastal plain in west Cumberland, is the most striking of all these monuments and is an essential element in the antiquarian's itinerary, as are the hogback tombstones here and at Lowther. The nearby churchyard cross at Irton, though it is Anglian rather than Scandinavian in origin, is also well worth seeing in its lonely churchyard away from any settlement but with a marvellous backdrop of the western fells. Much nearer the present, and somewhat less mystical, the monastic foundations of Shap and Calder Abbeys (and Furness, just outside the National Park) also deserve attention; Calder Abbey, beautifully sited in the valley pastures of the Calder, is especially attractive.

By any standards the foregoing is a remarkable catalogue of prospective interest and delight, yet it is still by no means comprehensive. The seeker after the quaint and the unusual will have noted the absence of the quirky, much-photographed Bridge House in Ambleside, for instance; the serious walker will have a special affection for scores of fells so far unmentioned; the literary tourist will have registered the omission of reference to Dove Cottage and other such magnets (though this will be remedied in a moment). The variety and the range of experience available to those prepared to use their eyes and uncover just a little of the meaning of the landscape is stupendous. Every dale has its own intrinsic attractions and its own subtly different character.

With this astonishing diversity of experience ready to be savoured, it is scarcely surprising that early tourists flocked to the area, even though in the beginning they came prepared to be assailed by feelings of fear and horror rather than wonder and excitement. Defoe saw Westmorland as 'the wildest, most barren and frightful' of English counties, but later in the eighteenth century the adherents of the Picturesque movement saw the Lake District in a new light. At first they came to write and paint, and then, with the aid of Father West's pioneering guidebook, published in 1778, they came to gaze. The guidebook sought out 'the soft, the rude, the romantic and the sublime' and directed the new tourists to 21 'stations', including Castle Head and Latrigg near Keswick and Red Brow on the western shore of Windermere. At these viewpoints the intrepid tourist would stand with his back to the scene and view it through a concave mirror – a 'Claude Glass' – which framed, reduced and perhaps slightly tamed the savage landscape.

The Lake District had already received some attention by the time West's guidebook was published, however. Not only Defoe but also Celia Fiennes had commented on the region, while the poet Thomas Gray visited the Lake District in October 1769. His *Journal in the Lakes* attracted the curious with its careful descriptions of selected spots, including Castlerigg, a 'Druid circle of large stones, one hundred and eight feet in diameter, the biggest not eight feet high, but most of them still erect'. Gray ventured no further into Borrowdale than Grange, and it was left to hardier souls altogether to explore the wild central mountains. The first of the Lake poets to conquer Scafell was Coleridge in 1802, in a celebrated expedition which involved a scrambling descent via the minor rock climb known as Broad Stand – still out of bounds to mere walkers today, and hence no mean achievement in the days before rock climbers had begun their exploration of the crags. Wordsworth arrived atop Scafell for the first time in 1818, though by this time his Lake poetry had gripped the imagination for more than two decades and his *Guide to the Lakes* was already in print.

Wordsworth, born in Cockermouth and educated in Hawkshead, returned to the Lake District in 1799, living successively at Dove Cottage, Allan Bank and the Parsonage during a fourteen-year interlude in Grasmere, and then settling at Rydal Mount from 1813 to 1850. His writings, though unquestionably both moving and compelling in places and often aptly descriptive of his native landscape, are highly embellished and romantic in style and certainly give little indication of the tenor of Lake District life; his sister Dorothy supplied unique insights into this aspect of the contemporary Lake District in her fascinating and extremely valuable *Journal*. Dove Cottage and Rydal Mount, in particular, have become Wordsworthian shrines and are seriously overcrowded in summer. Indeed the Wordsworth industry is now so prevalent in parts of the Lake District that it can be difficult to escape the commercialism and achieve a due sense of proportion in relating the poet to his landscape. Wordsworth's landscape was, after all, his own mental picture, a deliberate abstraction of reality rather than a detailed guide faithful to the precise pattern of fell and dale.

Wordsworth's decision to settle in the Lake District set the pattern for the poets of the picturesque, and he was soon followed by Coleridge and Southey, though neither attempted to capture the spirit of the region in their poetry. Coleridge lived only four years at Keswick, returning from time to time thereafter, but Southey stayed for forty years from 1803; he became Poet Laureate in 1813. Others to tread the fells included Thomas de Quincey, who succeeded Wordsworth in

Hill Top Farm at Near Sawrey, bought by Beatrix Potter in 1905 and now the most-visited home in the Lakes, despite the efforts of its present owners, the National Trust

Dove Cottage, John Keats, who climbed Skiddaw, and Charles Dickens and Wilkie Collins, whose rather more modest target was Carrock Fell. Sir Walter Scott's poem *The Bridal of Triermain* is set around the Castle Rock of Triermain, the remarkable rocky bastion at the southern end of St John's Vale. Amongst the painters to visit the district were J. M. W. Turner, whose *Morning Amongst the Coniston Fells* is a masterpiece, and Constable, who visited Borrowdale in the early years of the nineteenth century.

A much greater influence was that of John Ruskin, who regarded Keswick as 'a place almost too beautiful to live in' and eventually settled, in 1871, at Brantwood on the eastern shores of Coniston Water – where he was able to paint and sketch, write and philosophise whilst retreating in horror from the despoilation created by industrialisation. The house at Brantwood, with its spectacular view across the lake to the Old Man of Coniston, is open to the public and contains a considerable collection of Ruskin's paintings and other memorabilia. Another social reformer to settle in the Lake District was Harriet Martineau, whose *Description of the English Lakes*, published in 1858, had an enthusiastic audience. Novelists with a true feel for the region are rare – even the *Herries Chronicle*, the creation of Sir Hugh Walpole, who lived at Brackenburn on the slopes of Catbells, fails in this respect – and for the real flavour of the Lake District in fiction it is probably better to turn to the children's books of Beatrix Potter, whose Peter Rabbit series is quite clearly modelled closely on the immediate environs of her home at Hill Top in Near Sawrey.

This intellectual invasion in search of the picturesque and the aesthetically pleasing, spawning as it did a secondary invasion of tourists following in the footsteps of the guidebook writers, eventually prompted the realisation that landscape of the highest quality needed to be protected. External events played their part, too, with proposals for reservoirs and railways in the mountain core affronting the sensibilities of the Victorian environmentalists. Wordsworth's *Guide* had put forward the notion of the Lake District as 'a sort of national property', and threats to the right of men to enjoy that property, posed by proposals such as that to raise the level of Thirlmere to provide water for Manchester, saw an increasingly organised defence of the Lake District's landscape. The Thirlmere Defence Association, formed in 1877, lost its fight against the Mancunians but its founder, Canon Rawnsley (the incumbent of Crosthwaite parish near Keswick) went on to help establish the Lake District Defence Association in 1883, and later became a co-founder of the National Trust in 1895.

The formation of the Lake District Defence Association was prompted largely by the proposal to build a railway along the length of Ennerdale – an idea which would surely be laughed out of court in these more cost-conscious days. In fact the Ennerdale Railway Bill *was* lost largely because of financial problems, but the Buttermere Bill, possibly a more viable proposition, also fell in the face of concerted local opposition. Yet despite the growing realisation that control of development was urgently needed to conserve the Lake District, the area did not become a National Park until 1951. Since then the Park authority, the Lake District Special Planning Board, has sought to achieve its twin, and sometimes conflicting, aims of conservation and provision for recreation, in the face of pressure for development and for increased access, and despite periodic threats including those of greater afforestation and the further development of reservoirs. Always in the background, too, is the rapid growth of tourist pressure, in places now so intense that it can threaten to destroy the special features which attract tourists in the first place. Throughout all this, the authority has had to recognise its limitations, not just in terms of resources but in respect of land ownership (most of the National Park is privately owned) and lack of adequate control measures.

Pre-eminent amongst the major threats faced by the National Park was that of increased afforestation, following the excesses of the Forestry Commission in the inter-war period in locations such as Ennerdale, which was cloaked with an appalling shroud of conifers in the 1920s and is only now recovering. The outcry caused by this insensitive planting of great swathes of conifers has now largely died down as a result of major changes in outlook by the Forestry Commission which have greatly enhanced the quality of the landscape for present-day visitors. Most important, perhaps, was their acceptance of a ban on further planting within a widely defined area covering virtually the whole of the central fells – an agreement drawn up with the Council for the Preservation of Rural England in the 1930s and since policed very closely, to the great benefit of the landscape.

There have been other significant concessions from the foresters. Old-style planting in geometrical blocks has been largely superseded by amenity planting taking more account of the lie of the land and with a greater variety of species, and the increasing demands for recreational use of forests have brought a surprisingly willing and imaginative reaction, with visitor centres and forest trails in profusion. The centres in Grizedale and at Whinlatter are exemplary, and some of the forest walks are adventurous and full of interest, notably the Silurian Way in the Grizedale Forest Park. So although the ghost of earlier mistakes lives on, and obtrusive conifer plantations still mar the hillslopes above Thirlmere and to the north of Grisedale Pike and Hopegill Head, for instance, there is great hope for the future, and the opportunity given by clear-felling to improve the landscape has often been taken.

The reservoirs of the Lake District have been with us since 1885, when the Thirlmere dam was completed and the waters of the natural lake began to rise and envelop hamlets and farms such as Waterhead, The City and Yew House. Manchester's thirst for water was only temporarily slaked by this scheme, however, and in the 1930s Haweswater became the next target of the water engineers. The consequences for the quiet and secluded valley of Mardale, described by Bradley in the early twentieth century as 'unforgettable for the charm of its romantic beauty', were disastrous, for the level of the lake was raised by some 30m (95ft) and the village of Mardale Green and its former common field disappeared beneath its waters. Amongst the casualties were the church and the venerable Dun Bull Inn, twin focal points for the entire dale. The new landscape comprised a lake doubled in length and capable of unparalleled ugliness around its shores when its level was drawn down. Worse still, there is now no life in the dale, since the hotel which succeeded the Dun Bull is too far from the dalehead and the village itself was irreplaceable.

Other schemes have been less obtrusive. Whilst Seathwaite Tarn is obviously a reservoir (in this case for the towns of west Cumberland) the waters of Windermere have been harnessed to increase Manchester's supply still further without serious environmental consequences, and extraction from Ennerdale Water and even Wastwater has been small-scale and low-key to date. Nevertheless there have been other losses, such as the little-known valley of Wet Sleddale in the far eastern fells, and new schemes are still brought forward. The most objectionable of the recent crop was the proposal to increase the rate of extraction from Ennerdale Water and Wastwater to feed the Sellafield works; the lesson of Haweswater, with its dreadfully ugly bleached shoreline, has apparently still not been fully appreciated.

Greatly improved communications created a further challenge to the district from the eighteenth century onwards. Some idea of the considerable isolation of the area before the development of modern roads can be gained from the fact that until 1757 regular packhorse trains still left Kendal for London, and in the dales themselves packhorse routes such as those over Sty Head and between Borrowdale and Patterdale via Greenup Edge, Grasmere and Grisedale Pass were of crucial importance decades after this. The greatest legacy of the packhorse era is the survival of simple, low-arched packhorse bridges, including those at Stockley Beck in Borrowdale, New Bridge on the Walna Scar Road and Birks Bridge in upper Dunnerdale. The traditional route across the sands of Morecambe Bay was still used regularly in the eighteenth century – despite the inherent dangers of tides and quicksands – and a new service was introduced as late as 1781, with a light coach capable of carrying three passengers plying the route at a fare of five shillings. But by now the first turnpike routes were already in existence and it would not be long before a series of railways constructed around the fringes of the Lake District opened up the area yet further.

Twentieth-century tourism has affected the Lake District to a degree which would have astonished the early visitors with their Claude glasses and their horror of venturing far into the mountain recesses at the heart of the district. The easy accessibility of the district, mainly as a result of vastly increased car ownership and the construction of roads such as the M6, has resulted in an avalanche of visitors which has all but overwhelmed the tourist honeypots such as Grasmere, Ambleside and Bowness, and which has led to erosion on the most popular paths. Nevertheless, experienced Lakers can easily escape from the crowds, though they can only do so (and most are only too willing to do so) by forsaking the more obvious assets of the district such as Striding Edge and seeking out the less frequented but no less fascinating country away from the crowds.

The problem of erosion is a serious one, too, with paths being literally worn out by the passage of too many feet. Two examples from Great Langdale will suffice: the path from New Dungeon Ghyll to Stickle Tarn, substantially rebuilt for some hundreds of feet from valley level upwards, to such an extent that it resembles a staircase in places, and the broad highway leading up The Band from Stool End Farm to Three Tarns and Bowfell, where again enormous effort has had to be employed in restoring a path destroyed by walkers' boots. All too frequently paths are widened and deepened to such a degree that they even disfigure the distant views of the most attractive fells.

But the effect of tourism is not just to be seen in erosion of the most popular paths. It has much more fundamental effects too, on the economy of the area and the housing needs of local people. The congested roads of summer, particularly in places such as Ambleside, have posed apparently insuperable problems. In the case of Ambleside any bypass would be disastrous for the landscape, yet the existing roads are clearly inadequate to meet the demand. Grasmere, though its roads cope, has seen vast areas of land swallowed up in the creation of car parks. More worrying still has been the selective incursion of second-home owners into the specially attractive and accessible villages such as Hartsop and Troutbeck. Such places can be converted into part-time villages, almost deserted in midweek and throughout the winter, unable to sustain local services and providing the focus for fewer and fewer farming enterprises as farms are amalgamated and the demand for agricultural labour decreases. The sometimes astronomical rise in house prices in such villages means that locals are in any case unable to compete and – since the Planning Board rightly restricts the number of new houses being built – they have to move away from their local area.

All is not lost, however: though the Planning Board has been powerless to stop some of the unwelcome developments in this apparently gloomy catalogue it has had a hand in resisting certain incursions and it has been instrumental in conserving a great deal of the district's landscape simply by striving to keep the status quo. The highly encouraging result, as the succeeding chapters of this book illustrate, is that there is much to see and much to celebrate. The lakes are almost wholly unspoilt, yet between them cater where appropriate for a diverse cross-section including boating enthusiasts. The villages and towns, especially away from the accessible south-east, offer fascinating opportunities for exploration and a friendly welcome. There is a wealth of historic and literary associations and sites, and above all a network of rights of way that is so comprehensive that most dales can easily be explored on footpaths well away from roads. At a higher level the fells are almost without exception open to all, with an astonishing array of magnificent walking complemented by countless rock climbs of varied difficulty but consistently high quality. Ill-fated Rutland had the motto 'much in little'; richly deserved though this was, there can be little doubt that, given the remarkable quality and variety of the scenery of mountain and lake, it is a description which applies to the Lake District above all other districts in Britain.

2

ROCKS AND SCENERY

Two contrasting rock types between them determine the character of the majority of the mountain scenery of the Lake District: the Skiddaw Slates and the Borrowdale Volcanics. Other rocks, however, are locally important in helping to explain the landscape which we see today, and these include the Coniston Limestones, a band of weaker rocks which define some of the most important passes of southern Lakeland, and the Silurian series of shales and grits which form the gentle, rounded hills around Windermere. But whilst these rock formations explain the basic character of the landscape, the subsequent history of the rocks, and especially the effects of glaciation, have also had a profound influence on the final form of the landscape.

The Rock Types: Foundations of the Landscape

The northern Lake District is dominated by the **Skiddaw Slates**, the oldest rocks in the area. Skiddaw itself, neighbouring Blencathra and the Newlands fells are all composed of these ancient sedimentary rocks, formed in the muddy depths of the sea in the Ordovician period some 500 million years ago, and later hardened into slates, shales and fine-grained grits. Perhaps the character of the resulting landscape is best typified, however, by the gentle, grassy slopes of the Caldbeck and Uldale fells – the country commonly known as Back o' Skidda'. Here there is a succession of smooth, regular ridges with shaly debris

Skiddaw Slate country: the smooth north-western fells from above Buttermere church. The road across Newlands Hause to Keswick and Borrowdale can be seen to the right

moderating the angle of the steeper slopes and a surface cover of grass and heather on the gentler slopes. The group of Great and Little Sca Fells (nothing to do with their more illustrious namesake!), Meal Fell and Great Cockup is a fine example of this pattern of high, grassy and rather featureless sheepwalks, where the smallest landscape features of any worth – notably, in this case, the remarkably steep-sided trough of Trusmadoor between Meal Fell and Great Cockup – come as a surprise and indeed a delight to the explorer.

There are a number of exceptions to this general rule, of course. One is the High Stile ridge west of Buttermere and Crummock Water, which is uncharacteristically rugged, with towering crags ringing Birkness Comb; another is the crumbling face of Hobcarton Crag between Grisedale Pike and Hopegill Head in the north-western fells. And even in Back o' Skidda' country, there are dramatic contrasts to the smooth slopes already mentioned. The view from the crumbling walls of the hillfort on the summit of Carrock Fell may be dominated by rounded slopes such as those of The Knott, that dullest of mountains, but even here the massive, rocky back wall of the corrie containing

Bowscale Tarn is prominent across the valley of the Caldew, and in the distance the unmistakable outline of Foule Crag and Sharp Edge, those rocky bastions of Blencathra's summit plateau, is clearly in view. Nevertheless, the overall pattern is one of a subdued, rounded landscape, though even this is deceptive since Skiddaw is one of the four highest mountains in the Lake District.

Although the main outcrop runs from the north-eastern fringes of the Lake District through Skiddaw and Grasmoor to the smooth, lonely fells south of Ennerdale Water, the Skiddaw Slates also outcrop in some unlikely locations. The most far-flung is the remote block of fells in the extreme south-west of the Lake District – the massive whaleback of Black Combe and its satellites. This is an area of grassy, softly rounded fells, rarely visited except by explorers trekking across the flanks of Knott Hill to Swinside stone circle.

The dramatic difference between the scenery associated with the two major rock types is especially obvious in Borrowdale, the most varied of Lake District dales. Here the smooth slopes of the Catbells ridge, composed of Skiddaw slates, contrast vividly with the more broken, craggy character of the fells across the valley, to the east of Grange. Here the **Borrowdale Volcanics**, a series of solidified lavas and tuffs, have through their relative hardness and their reaction to erosion created a very different landscape. It is the landscape of the Scafell range, with dramatic cliffs such as Scafell Crag and the north wall of Great End, together with the bouldery summit plateau of Scafell Pike; of the Langdale Pikes, thrusting 600m (2,000ft) upwards from the flat valley floor of Great Langdale; and of Helvellyn, its western slopes surprisingly grassy and smooth (though unremittingly steep) but with dramatically craggy eastern approaches.

The eastern face of Dow Crag in the Coniston Fells illustrates many of the features of the Borrowdale Volcanics. The crags rise dramatically from above the rocky mountain tarn of Goat's Water, but they are separated from the tarn by substantial scree and boulder slopes, the product of later weathering of the rocks, and the crags themselves are far from uniform in appearance. Weaker bands of rock have been worn away to produce deeply-riven gullies, while the harder rock types form the five magnificent buttresses which, above all else on the crag, have attracted climbers for many years.

All across the central band of the Lake District there are supreme landscape features based on the Borrowdale Volcanics. In the west the Wastwater Screes, dropping steeply into the lake from near the summit of Illgill Head, provide the sternest, most intimidating backdrop to any

valley level scene, whilst the highest mountains in the district, Scafell
Pike and Scafell, dominate the head of the lake in concert with Great
Gable, symbol for the National Park and playground for early rock
athletes. The Napes Ridges here soar directly above the well-known
path from Wasdale across Sty Head to the upper reaches of Borrowdale;
the Napes Needle, of little account to the cragsman nowadays, was the
most famous of all the early climbs. More centrally, the Langdale Pikes,
where a particularly hard vein of tuffs was used by Neolithic man to
make stone axes, almost overhang Langdale, yet their northerly
neighbours are strangely unimpressive. In the east, the Helvellyn range
and Fairfield include classic examples of the rugged, knobbly fell
country characteristic of the Borrowdale Volcanics, not least with the
sharp summit ridge of St Sunday Crag and the wild, craggy recesses at
the head of Dovedale and Deepdale. And in the far east, too, the long,
lonely High Street ridge is based on the same rock series.

The **Coniston Limestone** series, separated from the Borrowdale
Volcanics by an unconformity, surfaces as a very narrow band running
north-east from the estuary of the Duddon through Coniston and across

*Great End and Aaron Crags from Seathwaite Bridge in Borrowdale: classic Borrowdale
Volcanics country*

the head of Windermere lake to Shap. Displaced from its true line in places by later faulting, this narrow outcrop nonetheless has a profound local influence on the landscape. The finest example, and one well known to walkers, is probably that of the Garburn Pass, where the Coniston Limestone has stood up less well to the ravages of time than the Borrowdale Volcanics to the north and Silurian shales to the south, and forms a low col utilised by a rutted, stony track following the old packhorse route from Troutbeck to Kentmere. East of Kentmere the pack trains negotiated a second col, still on the limestone (which can be seen in the field walls hereabouts), to reach Sadgill in Longsleddale. On the far side of the 18th-century packhorse bridge crossing the River Sprint is Stockdale Farm, where an old lime kiln in the farmyard is yet another clue to the presence of Coniston Limestone. The oldest beds in the series, coarse conglomerates and grits, were succeeded by fossil-bearing beds of limestone and shales, including the Ashgill Shales, blue fossiliferous slates named from the Ashgill Quarry on Torver High Common, west of Coniston.

The characteristically soft, subtle landscapes of the southern Lake District are derived from the **Silurian Series** of shales and grits which were deposited in a sea of fluctuating but increasingly shallow depth. The lowest beds, outcropping parallel to the Coniston Limestone, are the Stockdale Shales; above these a truly astonishing thickness of marine sediments was laid down – about 15,000 feet of Silurian sediments still remain and an unknown additional layer has been eroded away. The major beds are the Coniston Flags and the dull grey Bannisdale Slates, neither of them with a plentiful supply of fossils but with a few graptolites. The junction of the Silurian rocks with the Borrowdale Volcanics – albeit separated by the thin layer of Coniston Limestone – is everywhere dramatic, though nowhere more so than at Torver High Common, where the gentle moorland founded on the Silurian series gives way abruptly to the magnificent mountain scenery of the Coniston Fells, with the broad, rugged southern slopes of the Old Man of Coniston complemented by the plunging cliffs of Dow Crag. The southern landscape is not always totally subdued, however: within the vast thickness of the Silurian beds there are notable variations in resistance to erosion, so that little rocky tors stand out amongst low-lying basins, some of them containing minor tarns. Claife Heights, between Esthwaite Water and Lake· Windermere, is typically delightful; the easy but very pleasant walk from Near Sawrey to Wray Castle, for example, passes Moss Eccles Tarn and Wise Een Tarn and skirts the low rocks of Three Dubs Crags.

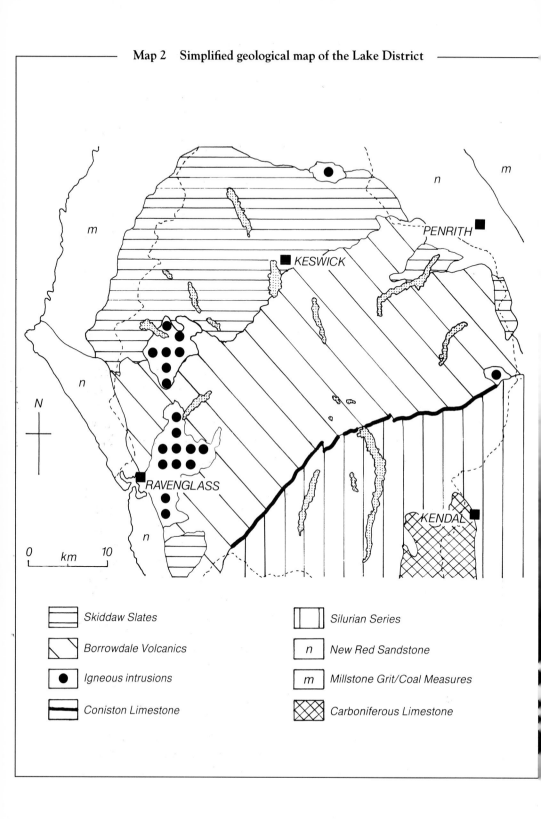

Map 2   Simplified geological map of the Lake District

N

0   km   10

KESWICK

PENRITH

RAVENGLASS

KENDAL

Skiddaw Slates

Borrowdale Volcanics

Igneous intrusions

Coniston Limestone

Silurian Series

n   New Red Sandstone

m   Millstone Grit/Coal Measures

Carboniferous Limestone

The end of the Silurian period was marked by a phase of folding and faulting during the 'Caledonian' period of mountain-building. The folding laid the basis for the present-day pattern of ridges and valleys, while faulting produced belts of weakened rock which were later eroded to form important through routes such as that over Dunmail Raise or passes such as Sty Head. In addition, in a number of areas igneous rock was intruded into the country rock, with marked effects on the scenery. The best known of the igneous intrusions, the Shap granite, nowadays affects the landscape chiefly because it has been voraciously quarried. The Eskdale granite has more subtle effects, producing an uneven, knobbly landscape of hillocks and hollows and, more intimately, drystone walls whose rounded pinkish boulders contrast vividly with the more angular, slaty volcanics. But the most spectacular contribution is that of the Ennerdale granophyre, a hard, pinkish columnar rock which forms the Red Pike to Starling Dodd ridge above Crummock Water, and also explains Scale Force, the highest waterfall in the Lake District, which drops 50 metres (170ft) in a magnificent single fall over the unusually resistant granophyre. Smaller igneous features are formed by the dykes, narrow sheets of once molten rock. Where these are more resistant than the country rock they form craggy rock faces; where the surrounding rock has proved less susceptible to erosion, the dykes now appear as gullies or cols. The most remarkable is Mickledore, the dramatic skyline notch separating Scafell and Scafell Pike.

Two further periods of mountain-building reshaped the geological picture of the Lake District: the Hercynian phase, which uplifted the Lake District into a dome and stripped off the recently deposited Carboniferous limestone, which still surrounds but does not penetrate into the Lakeland fells; and the Alpine phase, which once again raised the mountains and also superimposed the present radial drainage pattern. Still greater changes were to come, however, when the newly uplifted mountains were subjected to erosion by glaciers in successive Ice Ages, the first of them beginning about a million years ago. The results of glaciation are plainly visible in the Lake District landscape, and the next section describes these in more detail.

Glaciation: Moulding of the Landscape

The onset of the Quaternary period appears to have been heralded by increasingly severe winters, with heavy snowfalls, and summers so cold that the accumulating snow and ice never melted. The result was a series of glacial episodes, perhaps four in all, with the last glaciation occurring as recently as 10,000 years ago. When conditions were at their most severe it appears likely that virtually the whole of the Lake District was covered by ice, with only the highest peaks possibly escaping. As the grip of the Ice Ages lessened, the valley glaciers retreated until only the valley heads and in particular the corries immediately below the mountain tops were covered. Finally, the last of the ice – in corries on the north-east side of the main mountain systems – melted to leave a landscape much as we know it today, save for the more subtle and gradual changes which are still taking place.

The most pronounced effect of the glacial period was to produce deep valleys with steepened sides and, at the valley heads, rock basins below towering cliffs. These deep valleys are characteristically U-shaped in section as a result of gouging away of obstacles by the strong valley glaciers: obstacles such as interlocking spurs were simply eroded away. These ice-shorn spurs, steep and craggy, can be seen in many valleys, though perhaps the best scenically drop straight into the major lakes. Kailpot Crag and Silver Crag, jutting prominently into the Ullswater scene, are excellent examples. Representative U-shaped valleys include Great Langdale, where the northern valley slopes cascade some 600m (2,000ft) from the Langdale Pikes to the strikingly flat valley floor, but simpler, shorter and rather less well-known examples are probably even better representatives of the pure post-glacial form. Maybe the best of all is Riggindale, that cavernous bowl below the eastern ridge of High Street; the bare valley sides reach up to Kidsty Pike on one hand and to the Long Stile ridge on the other, while at the head of the valley steep, unstable slopes run up to the Straits of Riggindale, a narrow col separating Riggindale from the Hayeswater valley on the other side of the main ridge.

We should perhaps start an exploration of the landscape features associated with glaciation at the head of affairs, in the wild upland recesses of the valley heads. Here are the most dramatic glacial features of them all, the corrie basins – generally called coves in the Lake District – eating back into the heart of the major mountain systems. A common characteristic of these corries, many of which face north or east, is a tremendous back wall, an almost sheer cliff of naked rock gouged out by the rotational scouring action of the glacier ice. The scouring action also produced over-deepening of the floor of many corries, resulting in rock basins which often house a corrie tarn, that jewel of many a Lake District scene.

Red Tarn, tucked into the eastern slopes of Helvellyn, is a good

The deep U-shaped valley of Riggindale, a classic glacial form in the High Street range above Haweswater Reservoir. To the right are the eroded ridge of Long Stile and the waters of Blea Water, the deepest corrie lake in the district

illustration of these features: the rippling waters of the tarn in its rocky hollow are hemmed in by steep slopes rising to narrow ridges on two sides, and at the back by a forbidding craggy wall rising to the summit plateau of Helvellyn itself. Other fine examples are Goat's Water in the Coniston Fells, at the foot of the plunging buttresses and cascading scree fans of Dow Crag, and Bowscale Tarn, a little known corrie tarn in its dark bowl beneath the solid wall of Tarn Crag in the north-eastern slopes of Bowscale Fell near Mungrisdale. Bowscale Tarn, according to Victorian legend, was so deep and dark that even on a fine summer's day stars could be seen reflected in its waters, and it was also reputed to be the home of two immortal fish.

For a variety of reasons the number of tarns is less than was the case at the end of the last glacial period. In some cases man's intervention has proved disastrous: Keppelcove, in the Helvellyn range above Glen-ridding, became the reservoir for Greenside lead mine but broke its banks during a storm in 1927. The result is a green, flat marshy hollow which plainly proclaims its former status. In the eastern Lake District, where Blea Water (the deepest of all the tarns, with a maximum depth of 63m (207ft)) is a marvellous example of a corrie tarn in a cove with a spectacular back wall rising towards the summit of High Street, there is clear evidence below the surviving tarn of a second tarn at about 425m (1,400ft). Now there is just a boggy depression cultivated by rushes, though the clearest evidence is the moraine – glacial drift deposited at the edge of the ice – which still defines the natural dam whose temporary function was to hold back the waters of this lower tarn. Many corrie tarns, such as Levers Water in the Coniston Fells and Bowscale Tarn, are dammed by moraine piled up above the rock sill of the corrie, though others are penned back purely by the rocky lip of the corrie basin.

Where the headwalls of two corries were being extended back by ice action into opposing sides of the same ridge, progressive narrowing of the ridge took place. The result is the sensational scenery of places such as the Straits of Riggindale, where the valley heads of Hayeswater and Riggindale are divided by a narrow ridge used by the Romans for their spectacular road along the crest of the High Street ridge, and Threshthwaite Mouth, where the coves at the head of the Pasture Beck and Trout Beck valleys have eaten back into the ridge. In extreme cases the only remnant of the ridge is a desperately narrow arete, bare and rocky. The best known of these aretes is Striding Edge on Helvellyn, but they are perhaps best typified by Sharp Edge and Narrow Edge on Blencathra, and by the astonishing rocky ridge which connects Steeple, perched high above Ennerdale, to its parent mountain, Scoat Fell. This delicate ridge, its sides dropping precipitously into Mirklin Cove to the west and Mirk Cove to the east, must have deterred many peak-baggers coming upon it suddenly from the flat top of Scoat Fell. Sharp Edge, poised dramatically above the supposedly bottomless Scales Tarn, is even more challenging while Narrow Edge is broader but still a thrilling experience as well as a reminder of the power of ice to reshape the landscape.

Another upland feature is the hanging valley, often perched high above a major valley and with its stream cascading down over a steep rocky wall to the main valley floor. These valleys exist because of the differential erosive power of main valley glaciers – fed from a variety of sources and with the ability to scour down the valley floor to below sea level in places – and minor glaciers in side valleys, with only limited powers to gouge and erode. There are many fine examples of upland valleys abruptly ending at a rock step high above the major dales: in a number of cases the naming of a stream as Sour Milk Gill is a clear reference to the existence of a hanging valley above a tumbling, viscous cascade taking the beck down to valley level. Certainly this is the case in Borrowdale, where Gillercomb hangs above the main valley at

Seathwaite, and in the Buttermere valley, where the beck issuing from Bleaberry Tarn in its comb below Red Pike crashes down violently to the alluvial flats between Buttermere and Crummock Water. A further example of a hanging valley, again from Borrowdale, is that of Comb Gill, a wild upland recess unsuspected from its lower reaches above Thornythwaite Farm.

Where the hanging valley drops near-vertically to join its bigger brother the result, picturesquely in many cases, is a waterfall. Tourists flock to see some of them, notably Aira Force near Ullswater and Lodore Falls, where the Watendlath Beck emerges from a side valley hanging above Borrowdale – though here the difference in level is exaggerated because the Skiddaw Slates of the main valley have been eroded more swiftly than the Borrowdale Volcanics on which the Watendlath Beck valley is founded. Dalegarth Force in Eskdale, where Stanley Gill crashes 18m (60ft) over a rock step, is one of the finest waterfalls in the Lake District, and well worth a visit. The waterfall is enclosed in a narrow, wooded ravine which has now become the focal point of an excellent nature trail. A final example, very accessible and highly attractive, is Colwith Force, where the River Brathay drops from Little Langdale – another good example of a hanging valley – into Great Langdale.

Many of the glacial features in the valleys are associated with deposition rather than erosion, but one in-between feature, in terms of its location, is the ice-marginal channel, which occurs high up on the sides of a number of valleys. The most prominent is the channel separating Castle Crag in the Jaws of Borrowdale from the fellside above; this was probably formed by a stream running along the side of a glacier when the whole of mid-Borrowdale was filled with ice. Pre-historic man used the channel as part of the route beyond the Jaws into upper Borrowdale, and a Romano-British settlement evolved on the easily defended Castle Crag. Other ice-marginal channels occur on the slopes of High Doat nearby, on the western slopes of the Black Combe massif at Corney Fell, and very noticeably on the shoulders of Muncaster Fell, where streams taking the overflow from an Ice Age lake in Miterdale overflowed through channels scored into the granite fell at Ross's Camp and Chapel Hill.

In the valleys the most obvious features, apart from the general U shape and straightness of many dales, with their truncated, ice-plucked spurs, are of course the lakes. In the same way as the corrie tarns occupy rock hollows scoured out by the ice, these major lakes occupy overdeepened trenches which pay eloquent testimony to the erosive power of the valley glaciers. Even Derwentwater, long considered to be merely wide and shallow, has a mean depth of around 21m (70ft), while Crummock Water has a maximum depth of 44m (144ft) and the two long, narrow finger lakes in the Silurian hills, Coniston Water and Windermere, can comfortably top this. Perhaps these glaciers, confined in a narrow strip, plucked harder at the valley floors, for Coniston Water is up to 56m (184ft) deep and Windermere reaches 67m (219ft). Wastwater is not only the wildest in character but also the deepest of them all, with a maximum depth of 79m (258ft) – some 18m (58ft) below the level of the Irish Sea.

The extent and variety of the lakes is one of the greatest attractions of the Lake District; what is not immediately obvious, however, is that that extent has been steadily diminishing since the last glaciation, with the deposition of river silt and other material leading to the reduction in area of many lakes and the complete disappearance of others. Elterwater is a good example of a lake which was once much larger in area; its irregular reed-fringed shoreline is slowly being infilled, and the marshy lake flats around its feeder streams point to the gradual encroachment of silt and, in time, its disappearance from the landscape. This has already happened higher up Great Langdale, where the glacial lake above Chapel Stile has completely vanished. In Borrowdale, the shallow lake which spread around the middle of the valley near Rosthwaite must have been particularly attractive, with little islands such as The How, the rocky knoll close to the site of the present village. The erosive power of the River Derwent spelt the end of the lake, however, for the river cut the present gorge through the Jaws of Borrowdale and produced an escape route for the water which had been ponded back by a rock barrier.

In Eskdale, too, there is considerable evidence that the dale, a favourite with many despite its lack of water as a focal point, once boasted a number of lakes. Near the head of the valley, immediately below the brooding crags of Esk Buttress and the majestic face of Scafell Pike, the infant River Esk meanders through the flat bowl of Great Moss, where there was clearly a post-glacial lake of some magnitude. Eventually the Esk broke through the rock barrier below Green Crag, where the river now cascades down Esk Falls, to arrive at the second lake site, around Brotherilkeld. Once again the evidence is clear: terrace features around the fine seventeenth-century farmhouse define former lake beds, and there is even a fossilised river channel cut into one of the terraces. Lower down Eskdale, there were yet further lakes associated with the glacial period, when meltwater from the Eskdale glacier, whose snout perhaps reached as far as Eskdale Green in late glacial times, was trapped between the glacier itself and the tremendous sheet of ice which covered the Irish Sea region. Eventually water from both the Eskdale lake and the adjacent Lake Miterdale escaped through ice marginal channels and the water level was gradually reduced until the lakes were drained and Eskdale assumed its present character.

In a number of cases deposition by mid-valley streams has severed the original long finger lakes of the post-glacial period and produced valleys with two major lakes. In Borrowdale, Derwentwater and Bassenthwaite Lake were once one, but have been separated by the dumping of alluvial material from the River Greta on a bar of resistant rock. Deposition by the River Derwent is now insidiously reducing the extent of Derwentwater. The same pattern of an alluvial flat separating two lakes is apparent in Buttermere, where it is easy to imagine the winter torrents of Sour Milk Gill and Sail Beck bringing down boulders and other finer material to build up delta fans which progressively narrowed the central section of the lake before finally bringing about the present separation into Buttermere and Crummock Water.

The clearest evidence of glacial deposition lies in the heaps of debris which litter many of the Lake District's dales and mark the limits of valley glaciers at certain points in time. This glacial drift, or moraine, either lines the side of the valley or curves right across the valley. In the former instance, the lateral moraine forms hummocky areas of little hills and intervening hollows such as that in the deep trough of Mickleden in Great Langdale, or around Dunmail Raise at the highest point of the great through route of the Lake District, from Windermere to Keswick. In Borrowdale, too, there is glacial drift of this kind in the area between Seathwaite and Stockley Bridge, seen but not generally noticed by thousands of walkers each year as they make their way to Sty Head. And at the head of Deepdale, Wordsworth's 'craggy and gloomy abyss', fresh green mounds of recent moraine litter the valley floor.

The terminal moraines which mark the temporary end of the valley glaciers are perhaps of even greater interest. Examples can be drawn from most of the main valleys, from the far north-west, where a tree-topped ridge in the Cocker valley north of Lorton marks the point where debris from a melting glacier was deposited, to the far south-east, where a terminal moraine can be spotted just above the hamlet of Sadgill in Longsleddale; another former lake occupied the flat valley floor hereabouts. Lower down Longsleddale, the chapel just to the north of Ubarrow Hall, an ancient stronghold with a surviving pele tower, sits astride a moraine deposited during a glacial cold spell when the valley glacier advanced further down the dale. Back in Borrowdale, a series of morainic ridges around Rosthwaite indicates variations in the limits of the Borrowdale glacier as it waxed and waned. Thornythwaite Farm sits on the most impressive of these ridges of drift, but a number of others exist, including one which runs in a long curve from the Stonethwaite Beck to Borrowdale church, and which near Long-thwaite has been eroded by the river to reveal the amalgam of boulders, gravels and fine silts and clays dumped at the temporary edge of the glacier.

Amongst the minor landscape features associated with the glacial period the oddest are perhaps the erratics, boulders which were picked up by the ice and deposited large distances away, in areas where they were completely foreign to the country rock. The Bowder Stone, a 2,000 ton boulder perched in the Jaws of Borrowdale, is the most famous of these glacial erratics, though there are others which have travelled much further: boulders composed of rocks from the Borrowdale Volcanics series have been discovered as far south as Cheshire. Between the River Derwent and Rosthwaite, quite near the Bowder Stone, is an example of another glacial oddity, a roche moutonneé – a rock whose upstream surface has been smoothed by the passage of glacier ice but whose downstream face has been eroded away to form a craggy, uneven surface. The passage of the glaciers is also indicated by striations – grooves scratched out by rock trapped in the ice; there are examples of these scored rock surfaces in the dales, as in Mickleden, and also higher up – as high as 760m (2,500ft) on Scafell. And on the mountain summits, too, there are less dramatic but nevertheless fascinating indications of glaciation, including the stone polygons on the summits of Grasmoor, Skiddaw and Blencathra. This sorting of rock fragments by frost action, especially noticeable after a succession of sharp frosts in hard winters, is a reminder that the last glaciation was a mere 10,000 years ago, and that its effects are still very much with us.

3
PLANT AND ANIMAL LIFE

The complicated geological history of the Lake District, together with the extremes of climate to which the district is subjected, combine to produce a distinctive and diversified flora and hence an astonishing variety of wildlife habitats. This chapter summarises the characteristic flora and fauna in turn, before considering the question of nature conservation and describing a small selection of the very large number of nature walks which have been made available to allow observers to sample the riches available in the area.

Flora of the Summits and Corries

Consider the hurdles to be overcome by plants trying to establish themselves on the mountain tops of the Lake District. Snowfall can be expected from mid-September to May or even June, and in sheltered spots can lie for much of that time, and the chill factor from exposure to bitingly cold winds is considerable; one consequence is an extremely short growing season. Despite these problems, some plants do grow and the most tenacious of them thrive. The commonest are mosses, liverworts and lichens. One of the most unlikely is dwarf willow, often only 2½cm (1in) tall and with catkins less than a hundredth as long as that, but surviving in cracks and crevices amongst the crags, for instance those below Foule Crag and Sharp Edge on Blencathra and also on the eastern side of Fairfield and Helvellyn.

The crumbling face of Hobcarton Crag, a precious habitat for alpines, and the shapely summit slopes of Hopegill Head, seen across the forestry plantations of Thornthwaite Forest

Some protection from sheep is necessary for flowers such as alpine lady's-mantle, alpine saw-wort and the saxifrages, which ideally need water and the safety of ledges or gullies within crags or high corries. A real Lake District rarity, the red alpine catchfly, thrives in the safety of the crumbling, inaccessible cliffs of Hobcarton Crag, to the south-west of Grisedale Pike, where the Skiddaw Slates are threaded with quartz veins unusually rich in pyrites. A variety of ferns is also present in the uplands, especially where there is some shelter from the worst of the weather. Not surprisingly, several of the plants are relicts of the glacial interlude.

The Lower Fells

On the fellsides, and often in the wetter areas on the shoulders of the mountains, a somewhat more substantial flora exists, with bilberry, cranberry, and cloudberry together with a whole spectrum of the sphagnum mosses, varying from green to red in colour, in the wettest spots. These wet, marshy areas also have butterwort, which catches insects on its sticky leaves and then digests them, the equally insecti-vorous sundew, bog-rosemary, the golden-flowered bog asphodel and occasionally the rare bog orchid.

On drier slopes the commonest sight will be of grasses and, increasingly, bracken. The grasses include bent grasses and fescues, the staple diet of the ubiquitous sheep, and (in wetter locations) mat grass and rushes, whilst amongst the grass cover other plants thrive, notably the common tormentil with its delicate yellow flowers, sheep's sorrel and heath bedstraw. But bracken, with its long branched roots and dense cover, is likely to be encroaching everywhere except where the soils are thin or the young fronds are likely to be trampled on, especially on sheep tracks and footpaths. Controlling this fern is expensive and difficult, especially on broken rocky terrain, but control is vital if farms are to retain their fellside pastures. An equally intractable problem is over-grazing of the mountain pastures, which leads to a preponderance of mat grass and rushes, rejected as inedible by the sheep.

On crevices and ledges in the crags plants such as bilberry, its growth badly affected by grazing sheep in more open situations, bell heather and ling are likely to be found, whilst the scree slopes, which are too unstable for virtually all plants, do support the bright green parsley fern, rare outside the Lake District, named after the vegetable it resembles, and able to survive in crevices between the individual blocks of scree.

The Lakes and Dales

The meadowland which is now so characteristic of the dales is the successor to alder and willow woodland which (together with boulders in the wilder locations such as Wasdale Head) was cleared by the Norse settlers and has been prevented from regenerating. There is a striking contrast between the present enclosed in-bye fields, much improved and comparatively fertile, and the rough pasture on swampy and bouldery ground immediately beyond the intake walls. The meadow-land, visually so different from the unimproved land beyond the limits of farming, owes its appearance to the application of lime and fertiliser and above all to drainage. Without this it would revert to a swampy alder carr.

Sadly the meadows have been standardised in recent decades and many of them consist only of a stringently controlled mixture of hay grasses. Economic necessity has much reduced the incidence of plants such as the globe-flower and great burnet, though some species-rich

The Rusland valley between Coniston Water and Windermere, wholly unfamiliar to most Lakeland visitors

(right) Derwentwater and Blencathra from the lakeshore path at Brandlehow, close to the former lead mines. Brandlehow Park, bought in 1902, was one of the first purchases of the National Trust

meadows survive and provide a welcome splash of colour in a number of the dales, especially where wood cranesbill, windflower and (near Broughton, for example) daffodils are allowed to flourish as part of the grassland flora.

Plants of the dales include the sweet cicely, a pungent herb once used to disguise the flavour of dried meat, the Welsh poppy, the balsam (the yellow variety concentrated near Windermere) and the mealy primrose, which is widespread on the limestones of the southern Lake District. The 'mosses' formed on peat bogs around the margins of Morecambe Bay support a different vegetation, often now turning to pine or birch woodland – Rusland Moss (occupying what was once a shallow lake) and Roudsea Wood are examples. Finally, plants of the lake fringes include the common reed and tall herbs such as yellow loosestrife, together with the white water-lily, shoreweed and quillwort in shallow water.

Trees and Forestry

The prehistoric flora of much of the National Park was sessile oakwood, well adapted to the thin and acidic soils which are characteristic of the area. On soils derived from the encircling limestones, however, a richer flora based on ash, hazel, elm, lime and perhaps yew, with a varied ground cover, was common. Nearer the lakes and streams willow and alder were more likely to be present, while pine and birch dominated the poorer soils and the uplands. Today, much of this 'natural' broadleaved woodland has gone, and except where afforestation has taken place the higher ground can offer only single trees or small patches of woodland, with juniper shrubs (dwarf in exposed sites or at high altitude), rowan, holly, hawthorn and hazel predominant. The reasons for the loss of woodland are complex and include the effects of grazing by sheep and rabbits, burning to improve the quality and increase the quantity of pasture, and felling to provide the raw materials for the charcoal and woodland industries.

There is, however, still a substantial area of woodland – totalling about 10 per cent of the land area of the National Park – and this results from a number of initiatives. The role of the Forestry Commission in afforesting large areas is well known and formerly attracted much criticism, but they were preceded by 'romantic' landowners who

Waterslides in the valley of Mill Gill, one of the highlights of the walk from New Dungeon Ghyll to Stickle Tarn and the Langdale Pikes

replanted areas of open fell in the nineteenth century, notably with larch (on the slopes around Derwentwater and Buttermere, for example), and by the Manchester corporation, who planted spruce, Douglas fir and larch to reduce runoff and stabilise the slopes around their new reservoir of Thirlmere in the early years of the twentieth century.

The Forestry Commission's inter-war contribution was to plant large blocks of land in Grizedale, Ennerdale and around the Whinlatter Pass and elsewhere, and to do it unimaginatively and without much regard for its effects on the landscape. Public opposition to this large-scale and unsympathetic afforestation did, however, lead to an agreement between the Forestry Commission and the Council for the Protection of Rural England, under the terms of which the Commission agreed not to encroach further on the bare fellsides in the heart of the Lake District. The agreement has generally worked well and is still in effect, though one consequence has been to increase the rate of afforestation in the outlying fells.

The present-day broadleaved woodlands include one or two apparent survivals of the 'natural' woodlands, such as the Keskadale oaks, high on the stabilised scree slopes of a Newlands side valley, small and usually with multiple stems but possibly representing a remnant of the native forest; mixed woodlands such as those in High Furness, which include oak, ash, elm and birch, and which were often previously coppiced; and amenity woodlands, usually planted in the late eighteenth or early nineteenth centuries on the larger estates, where larch and beech are also represented. The means of ensuring the survival of these woodlands has become a matter of concern, and rightly so since they make a major contribution to the landscape quality of the Lake District.

The woodlands of Borrowdale are of special interest, so much so that some have attracted international attention. They are generally the descendants of woodland formerly exploited for timber or charcoal. A particularly fine example is Johnny Wood, between Seatoller and Rosthwaite and best approached across Folly Bridge, a fine packhorse bridge over the Derwent. It is protected as a Site of Special Scientific Interest, though a nature trail has been developed by the Lake District Naturalists Trust. The tree cover is predominantly oak, though the occasional larch is present together with patches of sycamore and shrubby rowan, holly and hazel. The wetter ground has largely been colonised by the more tolerant birch.

The special feature of Johnny Wood is the remarkable variety of

Map 3   Forestry and nature conservation

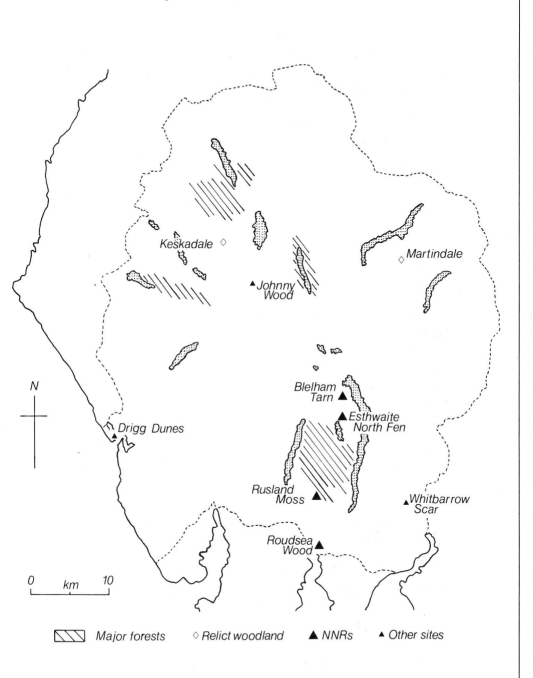

Keskadale ◇

Martindale ◇

▲ Johnny
Wood

N

Blelham
Tarn ▲

▲ Esthwaite
North Fen

◣ Drigg Dunes

Rusland
Moss ▲

▲ Whitbarrow
Scar

Roudsea ▲
Wood

0   km   10

| ⧄ Major forests | ◇ Relict woodland | ▲ NNRs | ▴ Other sites |

ferns, liverworts and mosses, wet habitat plants which succeed because the rainfall in this upper part of Borrowdale is so high. The ferns are predominant around rocky outcrops or where the floor of the oakwoods is bouldery or scree-laden, while the liverworts and mosses (mostly of species confined to the damp Atlantic coasts of Europe) do best on the thin, damp soils with high humidity provided by the dense canopy.

The typical woodland ground cover, especially in the mixed and amenity woodlands, is well illustrated by Hows Wood near Boot in Eskdale, acquired from the Forestry Commission by the Friends of the Lake District in 1986. The wood includes oak on rocky knolls, with a ground cover of bilberry and mosses, and larch, birch and sitka spruce with, especially on the fringes, a carpet of wood sorrel, common dog violet and creeping soft-grass. Other woods – and probably Hows Wood before the conifers were planted in 1970 – also support bluebells, primroses, wood anemones, foxgloves and meadowsweet.

Birds

The most interesting birds of the high fells are perhaps the buzzard, the raven and the golden eagle, preying on small animals and feeding on sheep carcases. Eagles were lost to the Lake District in the eighteenth century, but a nesting pair returned in the 1960s and the future looks hopeful. Buzzards, whose soaring flight is quite commonly witnessed by fellwalkers nowadays, became virtually extinct in the nineteenth century but survived in the Lake District because safe nesting sites could be found high in the crags. Merlin, preying on smaller birds, and kestrels and peregrine, nesting in the highest and most remote crags, are also present.

Amongst the smaller birds on the fellsides the meadow pipit and wheatear are commonest in summer, though skylarks, pied wagtails and ring ouzels are sighted frequently. Another common visitor to be seen flitting in and out of the bracken is the attractive yellowhammer. A bird characteristic of the high ridges is the dotterel, which feeds on flies and mountain spiders and beetles, and breeds only rarely in the Lake District, at 700m (2,300ft) or more on the bouldery, barren summit slopes of the high fells. The moorlands are home to the yellow plover and hen harrier.

In the Lake District's coniferous woodlands only the tits and goldcrests thrive, but in the oakwoods, which are lighter and have more abundant vegetation at lower levels, there is much more variety. The wood warbler, with its instantly recognisable song, the brown-tailed redstart, the tree pipit, the woodcock in limestone country and the pied flycatcher, quite rare in Britain but numerous in certain dales, especially in the south of the district, join the commonest woodland bird of all, the chaffinch. The lakes and rivers support a quite different bird population, notably the dipper, wren and grey wagtail in the lower valleys, and the common sandpiper and yellow wagtail near the lake shores. The lowland lakes support species such as the mallard, tufted duck and especially the merganser and also, in winter, the whooper swan. Upland lakes and tarns support fewer birds, though there are nesting pairs of the great crested grebe on Esthwaite Water and Blelham Tarn.

Along the Cumbrian coast there are some migrant waders such as the greenshank, spotted redshank and godwits, and there are colonies of gulls, particularly at the reserve at Drigg Dunes near Ravenglass and (outside the National Park) at Walney Island, where there are eiders and lesser black-backed gulls. At Drigg, the Ravenglass Gullery and Nature Reserve (access by permit only) has a substantial colony of great black-headed gulls.

Butterflies and Moths

Though the fells of the Lake District are not particularly rich in butterflies or day-flying moths, the peripheral limestone hills and the Cumbrian coast support a much wider variety, and there are occasional gems in the Lake District proper. The best is perhaps the mountain ringlet, dark brown with orange markings, which feeds on mat-grass and occurs only in the Lake District and a small area in the Scottish Highlands. It is only likely to be seen during sunny spells in June and July, and even then only above 550m (1,800ft); amongst the most likely places for sightings are Red Screes and the Langdale fells. The only other butterfly breeding in the high fell country is the small heath, which is common throughout Britain. At lower levels the meadow brown, green veined white and common blue are relatively numerous and easily spotted. The commonest moth in mountain country is the yellow and black wood tiger, though the grey mountain carpet and the red carpet may also be seen. At lower altitudes the commonest wood-land moths are nocturnal and there are few moths likely to be spotted.

The limestone hills in the southern Lake District, and especially those around Underbarrow (where there are patches of limestone pavement on the top of Underbarrow Scar) and Witherslack, are home to a much wider range of species. Four fritillaries (the high brown, pearl-

The hidden valleys east of Ullswater, home to the Martindale deer forest. This view shows Martindale and The Nab

bordered, small pearl-bordered and the scarce dark green) can be seen, together with the northern brown argus and the northern brown, the last named at its southern limit in Britain. The darting grayling, dark brown and rather large, can be seen here and also in the coastal sand dunes of Furness. The most interesting of the many moths is the fast-flying least minor, which occurs only here and in a small part of western Ireland. More widely distributed is the six-spot burnet, a red and black moth likely to be sighted both in the limestone hills and in the coastal strip. The emperor moth and northern eggar are both to be seen in the heather moorland.

Mammals

Though the commonest mammal in the Lake District is the field vole, which thrives in all habitats from the deepest valley to the bleakest mountain top, the mammals most likely to be seen by the casual visitor are the rabbits and, perhaps surprisingly, deer. The red deer, the largest of the mammals, is concentrated in Grizedale Forest, where the Forestry Commission controls its destiny, and Martindale. In the latter location the preservation of the species has been achieved first by the area's medieval designation as a deer park and more recently by virtually excluding visitors from the remote eastern fells where it thrives. It can, however, sometimes be spotted roaming more widely in the fells east of Ullswater. Roe deer are more widespread and can be encountered in any of the woodlands or in the adjacent bracken or heather.

The Lake District is one of the last refuges of the red squirrel – its grey cousin, thankfully, has only rarely been noted making incursions – and followers of woodland walks, notably in the coniferous plantations of Furness, will often be rewarded with a sighting. Other mammals which are often seen include the badger, very common and best seen in the woods at twilight, foxes, shrews and water voles. Foxes can often be seen (or heard) on the fellsides, though they are more at home in the rocky crevices in crags or scree. A number of mammals have, sadly, become much less common, including the dormouse, otter, pine marten (which may exist amongst the conifers, as in Grizedale Forest, or even above the treeline) and mountain hare. Finally, mention should be made of the bat, six species of which survive in the Lake District – the pipistrelle, long-eared, natterer's, noctule, whiskered and doubleton's.

Reptiles

Though few of them will be apparent to the casual observer – and one or two would be repellent if they were! – ten of the twelve reptiles and amphibians native to Britain are present in the Lake District. Two snakes (the grass snake and the adder or northern viper), a lizard and a slow worm comprise the reptiles, while amphibians are represented by three newts, two toads and a frog.

The grass snake, which can be either brown or green but has a black-bordered yellow or white collar, has the distinction of being the larger of the two Lakeland snakes. It is aquatic, often gathering its food supply underwater, and can also climb vegetation. The adder, recognisable from the zigzag markings along its back, is rare and despite its reputation is unlikely to attack unless provoked. The other Lake District reptiles are the common lizard and the slow worm, a smooth and legless lizard rather similar to a snake, which often falls prey to hedgehogs and adders.

The three newts, in descending order of size, are the warty or great crested newt, the common newt and the palmate newt, which is the most numerous in the district. The common toad is also present in the Lake District in very considerable numbers, whilst the natterjack or running toad – a poor swimmer which, whilst it is comparatively rare, can often be found in burrows in the sand dunes along the west Cumberland coast – and the common frog, which can be found

Haweswater Reservoir, an ugly intrusion into the Mardale valley but one of the few homes of the schelly, from the slopes of Harter Fell

throughout the district from the dale bottoms almost to the mountain tops, complete the roll call of amphibians.

Fishes

The commonest fish in the Lake District is probably the trout, which is in nearly all the lakes and in the becks and rivers. The only other fish which inhabits both the rich, silty, reed-fringed lakes of the agricultural lowlands and also the rocky and less food-rich upland lakes and tarns is the char, though the perch is also widespread. There are also two fish found only in the Lake District – the schelly and the Cumberland vendace.

The trout include brown trout, characteristic of the lakes and becks, and sea trout and indeed salmon, which migrate up the rivers to spawn. The biggest, usually found in the major lakes, grow to about 60cm (2ft) in length and include perch, sticklebacks and minnows in their diet; the smallest are less than half that size and are more likely to feed on insects, crustacea and plankton. The char is quite similar in appearance and behaviour, though it is commonest in deep, rocky lakes such as Wastwater, Ennerdale Water and Buttermere, and in mountain tarns such as Goat's Water high in the Coniston Fells, where it was introduced by man. Potted char is a celebrated Cumbrian delicacy.

Of the fish which are more likely to be encountered in the reedy, silty lakes the perch and pike are the most important. The perch, with its pink fins and dark stripes, generally feeds on small animals and plankton and is numerous in lakes such as Esthwaite Water, while the pike is a more voracious carnivore, eating trout, char and perch. Not surprisingly the largest pike are big, occasionally weighing 30lb or more. Amongst the smaller fish are minnows, which usually congregate at lake edges, both in lowland lakes and in corrie tarns such as Grisedale Tarn, stone loach and bullheads, which are common in the becks, sticklebacks and eels, which are very widespread.

The schelly is found only in two lakes, Ullswater and Haweswater, and one tarn, Red Tarn high on the eastern flanks of Helvellyn. It grows to about 35cm (14in) in length, feeds on plankton and is silvery in colour. Though it is quite common in Ullswater it is not often seen and is rarely netted by fishermen. The Cumberland vendace, which is from the same family as the schelly, lives only in Derwentwater and Bassenthwaite Lake. It is a pale silver colour underneath, but blue-grey above, and grows only to about 20cm (8in). Again, although it is numerous, it is comparatively rarely seen. Even less likely to be seen is a small freshwater shrimp, mysis relicta, a glacial relict found only in Ennerdale Water.

Conservation

The range and variety of natural habitats in the Lake District is impressively large, and as a consequence the flora and fauna they support is also considerable. Inevitably it is under threat, and not just from the weight of visitor numbers and the illegal activities of a few who specialise in activities such as robbing nesting sites. The conservation of the plant and animal life of the district is therefore a matter of very proper concern.

A great deal has been achieved, partly through statutory means with the designation of the most important and most vulnerable sites, and partly through the education of visitors and co-operation from interest groups such as rock climbers – increasingly aware of the need to avoid disturbing nesting birds on the crags – and boating enthusiasts, whose activities on the lakes sometimes have to be curbed in order to allow wildlife to survive. The zoning of Bassenthwaite Lake is a good example of the scope for co-existence.

Designation of sites where nature conservation is a priority can take a

A spectacular area of limestone pavement on the summit of Whitbarrow Scar

number of forms. The Nature Conservancy Council has the responsibility for designating Sites of Special Scientific Interest, and by 1986 had designated 68 such sites. The NCC had by then also designated four areas as National Nature Reserves, though there are numerous other candidates which would merit similar status but which through lack of resources have not been designated. Partly in recognition of this, local bodies have been active in nature conservation, and 13 local nature reserves have been established, the majority of them by the Cumbria Trust for Nature Conservation, an extremely energetic voluntary body.

Amongst the most important of the National Nature Reserves is the site at Roudsea Wood, in the extreme south of the National Park near Haverthwaite, accessible on rights of way only except by permit but nevertheless quite fascinating. A shallow valley divides ridges of Bannisdale slate and carboniferous limestone, giving acid woodland on the former with oak and birch much in evidence; lime-rich woodland on the latter, based on ash and hazel but also with sycamore, wild cherry, crab apple and yew, and with a profusion of plants such as columbine, bird's-nest orchid and lily of the valley; and, in between, a marshy valley colonised by sedges and containing a small tarn. The fauna includes roe deer, red squirrels and badgers.

Rusland Moss National Nature Reserve, in the highly attractive valley of the Rusland Pool between Coniston Water and Windermere, is a fine example of a raised bog formed over the site of a shallow lake which was gradually silted up and invaded by successive waves of vegetation, culminating in the present thick pine woodland cover on the drying peat. The pine at Rusland Moss was the source of seed for many of the seventeenth- and eighteenth-century pine plantations of the Lake District, and is demonstrably a different species to the much more widespread Scots pine.

At Esthwaite North Fen (Priest Pot) a typical fen habitat has developed on alluvium deposited where the Black Beck enters what was, until it was separated from the lake by silting up, the head of Esthwáite Water. The four-acre site is in the slow process of transition from open water through fen to damp woodland, with the fen colonising the remaining waters of Priest Pot at a rate of about 20cm (8in) a year over the last century. The vegetation includes water lilies rooted in the banks built up by the Black Beck, bullrushes on the recently colonised reed-swamp and sedges on the slightly drier ground. Alder and willow are also present here and represent the first signs of woodland regeneration; oak and hazel are also now well established in places.

Blelham Tarn, west of Windermere, has long been used as a field research station; in addition to the tarn the reserve consists of a sphagnum bog and wet willow woodland. The tarn is home to trout, perch and pike and the great crested grebe nests there. The bog is sited over two small infilled glacial kettleholes (hollows formed by the delayed melting of ice blocks) and the site has developed from open water through peaty fen and then carr to its present status. In the nineteenth century turbary (peat-cutting) rights were exercised; now there is a rich variety of habitats to be protected, with plant communities representative of wet woodland, fen and sphagnum bog.

At Drigg Dunes, near Ravenglass, the gullery (a local nature reserve) has a breeding colony of black-headed gulls together with a consider-able variety of other seabirds, including terns, oystercatchers and ringed plover, and wildfowl such as the now-ubiquitous red-breasted merganser and the shelduck. Snipe and lapwing populate the estuarine marshes, while adders are plentiful, and both toads and newts breed in the freshwater ponds. The flora, where it has colonised the dunes, includes sea spurge, sea bindweed, carline thistle and bloody cranesbill, and on the shingle includes the unusual Isle of Man cabbage.

Whilst these sites are of exceptional importance because of the flora and sometimes the fauna they support, access to them is inevitably and quite rightly restricted and sites of more localised importance may well be of greater significance to the amateur naturalist or the interested layman. The second category of visitor is especially well catered for nowadays, with a burgeoning number of nature trails designed to introduce the district's habitats to a wider cross-section of the public.

A selection of these nature trails must include that at Claife Heights, where a circular walk has been laid out in broadleaved woodland to the west of Windermere by the National Trust; the pied flycatcher and a variety of waterside birds are among the attractions. The Trust is also responsible for the nature trails at Friar's Crag, a well-known beauty spot near Keswick, and Loughrigg Fell, where a particularly varied nature walk passes through woods, farmland and fellside and also follows the course of a beck for some distance. Amongst the Cumbria Trust for Nature Conservation's contributions is the Nether Wasdale nature trail, a 5km (3 mile) walk partly alongside Wastwater, where the rapidly increasing population of the red-breasted merganser is likely to be seen, together with mallards and the common sandpiper, and partly through woodland and peat bog.

More specialised interests are catered for by the Forestry Commission, which has established a number of observation towers and hides within its forests. The tower (access by prior arrangement) at Spruce Knott in Grizedale Forest, well placed to view the activity of the wildfowl on Wood Moss Tarn (where both red and roe deer are also frequent visitors), is a good example. A different kind of experience is offered at Whitbarrow Scar, near Witherslack in the south-eastern Lake District, where there is access on public rights of way to a nature reserve which includes a substantial area of limestone pavement, abruptly terminated to the west by crags and screes. The reserve is a haven for breeding birds and there are red and roe deer in the woodland areas, whilst the flora is characteristic of limestone country, based on juniper, ash and birch. As with all these sites, Whitbarrow gives yet another indication of the diversity of the natural habitats in the National Park and of the efforts being made to conserve them.

4
ANCIENT LANDSCAPES

The Lake District is fortunate in having a good many ancient monuments which, in these days of the leisure 'industry', have become outstanding tourist attractions. The stone circle at Castlerigg near Keswick, with its stupendous view of the mountains on all sides, has become the destination of coach parties touring the Lakes; the Roman fort of Hardknott is a popular port of call for tourists in upper Eskdale; and the medieval pele towers at Muncaster, Dacre and elsewhere are familiar sights. But the context within which these well-known features are set is a great deal less familiar. Questions such as: why are they situated where they are? when were they constructed? and why? are sometimes not easily answered. Some idea of the answers is, however, invaluable in setting the scene for visits, highly entertaining as well as educational, to some of the many prehistoric, Roman and medieval survivals in the district.

The Lake District in Prehistoric Times

If the casual visitor to Ullswater, with half a day to spare at Pooley Bridge, takes the lane beside the church and walks south-eastwards towards Heltonhead for about a mile he will find himself on Moor Divock, superficially just an upland sheep pasture overrun with bracken, best known for the fine view of the Helvellyn range across the lake and, to the east, a distant prospect of the Pennines across the Eden

Map 4   The prehistoric and Roman Lake District

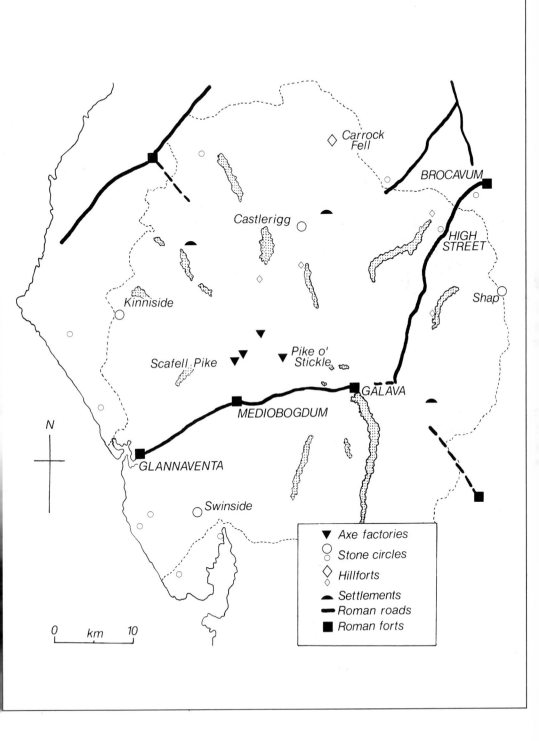

Carrock
Fell

BROCAVUM

Castlerigg

HIGH
STREET

Kinniside

Shap

Scafell Pike

Pike o'
Stickle

GALAVA

MEDIOBOGDUM

N

GLANNAVENTA

Swinside

▼ Axe factories
○ Stone circles
◇ Hillforts
◖ Settlements
▬ Roman roads
■ Roman forts

0   km   10

The remarkable remains of a cairn circle on the slopes of Moor Divock, to the east of Ullswater

valley. But there is a great deal more to this area, and it is readily available to those willing to scratch just a little below the surface.

The broad track crossing the Heltonhead path, for example, lies on the line of High Street, the spectacular Roman road from Brocavum, the fort outside Penrith, across the High Street range to Galava (Ambleside). Yet the Roman soldiers were by no means tramping virgin territory when they came this way. Just to the right of the Heltonhead path is The Cockpit, a stone circle giving a clear indication of the importance of this area before the Romans came; and to the left is its smaller brother, an unusually attractive and very well preserved cairn circle, and the Cop Stone, sole survivor of another prehistoric monument. It soon becomes apparent that the whole area is thickly populated with such features, and with other unexplained bumps and hollows.

This is a severe setback for the theory that the Lake District was regarded as of such little value in ancient times that it was largely left alone until the Viking settlers peopled the dales from the ninth century onwards. Everyone knows, of course, of the stone axe factory on Pike o' Stickle in Great Langdale, and of the Roman forts at Galava and, more spectacularly, Hardknott at the head of Eskdale, but it now seems that it is wrong to regard them as exceptional incursions into the heart of

Ullswater from the slopes of Birkhouse Moor

mountain country. The rash of burial mounds on Stockdale Moor, on the lonely fells between Wasdale and Ennerdale, and the settlements, possibly of the Romano-British era, on Threlkeld Knotts, Lanthwaite Green – on the shores of Crummock Water – and Millrigg (Kentmere) combine with the hillforts on Carrock Fell and in Borrowdale, Mardale and above Thirlmere to provide persuasive evidence of the peopling of the prehistoric Lake District.

Perhaps the best scientific evidence, however, is the unspectacular, painstaking but thorough research into forest clearance and agricultural cultivation by Neolithic man at sites such as Devoke Water, in its upland basin between Eskdale and Dunnerdale, and Ehenside Tarn, near Beckermet on the coastal plain south of Egremont. The Neolithic peoples, who had reached the Lake fringes by about 4000BC, were essentially farmers, with the ability to rear animals and grow cereals. They needed room to farm, however, and their major contribution to the landscape was large-scale clearance of the forests which had, since the end of the last Ice Age, colonised the uplands. Analysis of pollen trapped in the silts deposited in tarn beds has established that the forest cover was unbroken in about 5000BC; but Neolithic man, spreading inland from early flint-working sites near the west Cumbria coast, was soon felling the trees and establishing zones of agricultural cultivation. Mounds of cleared stones near Devoke Water offer telling visual corroboration of the pollen analysis in this respect.

The settlement at Ehenside Tarn, discovered accidentally during ploughing in the nineteenth century, revealed Neolithic pottery, a stone quern for grinding the corn which was cultivated in the surrounding fields, wooden objects such as a dug-out canoe with its paddle, and several stone axes. The axes, a light greyish green in colour, came from volcanic tuffs in the Borrowdale Volcanics series, and their source has been established as one of the several stone axe 'factories' in the central fells of the Lake District – on Scafell and Scafell Pike, Great End, Glaramara and, the most dramatic site of all, on Pike o' Stickle, towering above the flat valley floor of Great Langdale.

The Pike o' Stickle axe factory, situated in a scree gully just below the summit of the mountain, is clearly seen from the valley but rather more difficult to reach across rivers of steep and unstable scree. Given that there are serious problems of erosion here, and that the roughly

The Grasmoor fells from one of the gullies above Eel Crags, high on the Newlands slopes of Maiden Moor

shaped flakes (which were polished and trimmed at lower altitudes) are difficult to identify amongst the scree, close inspection is in any case not recommended. But even the most distant view is inspiring, not only because of the exposed, high-altitude nature of the site but also because of the organisational abilities which are implied, for these Langdale rough-outs were transported to finishing and polishing sites and then exported to the rest of Britain – Lake District axes having been found in the Isle of Man, the Yorkshire Dales and much further south, in Gloucestershire and on the coast of southern England.

The discovery of these stone axe factories, and of the settlements at lower levels, has confounded earlier ideas about the use made of the mountains in prehistoric times. No longer can it be assumed that the great monuments such as the Castlerigg stone circle were erected by a people who had no knowledge of the surrounding mountains; indeed, it is now clear that they had explored them thoroughly and exploited their wealth where possible. As a result, many of the tracks which run into the remote daleheads or connect adjacent valleys over passes such as Sty Head and Esk Hause can now be considered as prehistoric trade routes in their own right.

The stone circles, however, must still be counted amongst the most evocative survivals of the Neolithic age. The best-known is Castlerigg, though the best is perhaps Swinside on the seldom visited slopes of Black Combe. The Castlerigg circle consists of 38 stones, with a further ten inside the circle. Its purpose is unknown but in the northern arc of the circle there is an identifiable entrance, similar to that in the henge monument at Mayburgh, near Penrith. Worth seeing for its own sake, the circle also stands in one of the most attractive locations in the northern Lake District, with breathtaking views of the brooding mass of Skiddaw, the corrugated southern face of Blencathra, the craggy northern outliers of the Helvellyn range, and – across the unseen Derwentwater – the attractively grouped Grasmoor fells.

In the far south-west is a sight not to be missed, the Swinside stone circle, with some 55 surviving stones and a diameter of about 150 feet. Sited on a grassy moorland plateau on the lower slopes of Black Combe, it is an outstanding example of this class of monument, at its best on a clear day in spring, perhaps with the snow-capped blue line of the higher fells in the distance. On the eastern fringes the scanty remains of a stone circle, much damaged by the building of the railway, still stand at Shap in conjunction with a series of standing stones which appear to represent the surviving remnants of a stone avenue extending to some two miles in length. Other circles exist at Moor Divock, as already mentioned, and possibly at Kinniside, south of Ennerdale Bridge, though the longevity of this particular example is open to doubt.

Neolithic burial places are represented by the long barrow of Sampson's Bratful on Stockdale Moor, now a remarkably remote area above the headwaters of Worm Gill, between Ennerdale and Wasdale, but clearly a place of considerable prehistoric importance. In addition to the long mound of Sampson's Bratful, some 29m (96ft) in length and 13m (44ft) across, the surrounding moor contains numerous other prehistoric cairns, all standing within an area which later became part of a medieval deer park and is now an upland sheep pasture. Best approached by the monks' road from the Cold Fell gate on the moor road between Ennerdale Bridge and Calder Bridge, passing close to Matty Benn's Bridge (a classic single-arched packhorse bridge now in disuse), Stockdale Moor amply rewards the seeker after solitude.

Most of the burial mounds, however, are of Bronze Age date, including the round barrows clustered on Burnmoor, between Wasdale and Eskdale – the walk between the two dales, passing close to the barrows and alongside Burnmoor Tarn, is a delightful and easy expedition – and in areas such as Moor Divock, that prehistoric metropolis, and Banniside Moor near Coniston. This latter area is thickly populated with round barrows, though not quite so much as the environs of Devoke Water, where more than 1,200 barrows have been identified. Dunmail Raise, the round barrow which has also given its name to the pass carrying the main route through the Lake District, is perhaps the best known of these burial mounds, though its attribution to the Norse King Dunmail is apocryphal.

There is only one substantial example of that most typical survival of the Iron Age, the hillfort, within the boundaries of the National Park. This is the fort which, somewhat improbably, crowns the summit of Carrock Fell, the most easterly fell of 2,000ft or more in the northern Lake District. The remains are substantial and very well worth the stiff climb from the hamlet of Mosedale. The walls of the fort still stand to a height of several feet in places and the remains of gateways are still discernible. The fort, which covered an area of about five acres, was probably slighted by the Romans soon after they gained control of the area.

Several smaller Iron Age hillforts – generally rather rough-and-ready enclosures defended by single ramparts and perhaps ditches – have been identified in the Lake District. Perhaps the most accessible is Castle Crag in Borrowdale, spectacularly sited on a rocky tor in the Jaws of Borrowdale and with excellent views down the valley to

Derwentwater. The fort, with its crumbling ramparts, is difficult to date, and of uncertain purpose, but fragments of Roman pottery have been discovered on the site. Another delightfully situated hillfort, again probably late Iron Age in date, is also sometimes known as Castle Crag, though it actually lies on Birks Crag above the upper reaches of Haweswater. Still further small defended enclosures of this type include those on Shoulthwaite Crag near Thirlmere and on Dunmallet Hill at the foot of Ullswater.

Slightly later in date than these defensive enclosures, possibly spanning the period of the late Iron Age and the Roman occupation, are the unenclosed settlements such as Threlkeld Knotts, to the east of Keswick; Lanthwaite Green, near Buttermere; and Millrigg, in the Kentmere valley. These settlements were clearly occupied in times of relative peace, since the hut foundations appear to be those of farmers and the clusters of houses were surrounded by a few fields roughly marked out with stone walls, probably to herd cattle. The site at Threlkeld Knotts is a good example, with the remains of four or five hut circles and the boundary walls of several roughly rectangular fields faintly picked out in wiry grass and heather on a level shelf above the Glenderamackin valley. At Lanthwaite Green, too, the fascinating remains of trackways, hut circles and boundary walls can be picked out on level ground below the steepening slopes of Grasmoor at the foot of Crummock Water. Some at least of these settlements were occupied after the Romans arrived in the Lake District, and it is to the Romans that we now turn for the next strand in the history of the area's landscape.

The Romans

Once they had brushed aside initial resistance to their invasion of Britain in 43AD the Romans advanced northwards at considerable speed, reaching the fringes of the Lake District less than 40 years later. They moved only selectively into the region, however, and the main evidence of their occupation is associated with one road and a number of associated forts. They were more active in the Eden valley, immediately to the east, and the Lake District and west Cumbrian coast served largely as a buffer zone within which attacks from Scotland or

A delightful footpath now follows the line of High Street, the Roman road across the mountain range of the same name, through the Trout Beck valley east of Ambleside. The Ill Bell group of fells forms the background

Ireland could be contained or, as in the case of the Roman ports such as Ravenglass, as possible launching pads for the invasion of Ireland: an invasion which never actually took place.

The one Roman road of real importance in the Lake District proper was High Street, running from Brocavum near Penrith to Galava (Ambleside), together with its extension westwards across the Wrynose and Hardknott Passes to the port at Glannaventa (Ravenglass). From the first the Romans must have recognised that the chosen route was one which would present considerable difficulties because of its exposure and elevation – reaching over 2,700ft on the High Street ridge whose name it shares – despite the fact that there appears to have been a pre-existing British trackway along the ridge. Nevertheless they persevered, and the result is an extraordinary and very well-defined route along the crest of the ridge, from Celleron Farm, a few miles south-west of Penrith, to the Trout Beck valley and (by means of a traverse of Wansfell, where the exact Roman route is uncertain) the remains of the fort at Galava.

There are few more varied and worthwhile long-distance routes in the National Park than the 'Roman' route from Penrith to Ravenglass, and it is worth dwelling on the details of the journey, some of which can be followed by car but which will appeal most to walkers, who can enjoy a magnificent walk. From Celleron, where the tarmac ends, the route lies across Heughscar Hill to Moor Divock, already noted as a centre of prehistoric activity. The very fact that the Roman road appears to head for the stone circle at The Cockpit, altering course after passing the ancient monument, underlines the fact that this was not a newly-devised route but an adaptation of an existing thoroughfare. From The Cockpit the line of the Roman road can easily be followed as it rises inexorably onto the most easterly ridge of the Lakeland mountains, passing over Loadpot Hill, Wether Hill and High Raise on its way southwards to the narrow col of the Straits of Riggindale and then the level plateau of High Street itself. The route reaches the Trout Beck valley by descending Scot Rake, named after the border raiders who caused medieval havoc in these parts, and crosses Wansfell to arrive at the fort of Galava on low-lying ground at the head of Windermere.

The line of the Roman road westwards from Galava through Little Langdale can be traced only with difficulty, but as it crosses the Wrynose Pass the Roman road can again be detected – not always using the same alignment as the present tortuous motor road – and west of Cockley Bridge it is very clearly seen. At first the track to Black Hall, a straight and very Roman-style route, marks the way, but after reaching

The substantial remains of the walls of Hardknott Roman fort, backed by the great fells at the head of Eskdale

the farmhouse the route becomes much more devious, climbing in a series of zigzags and at one stage cutting through bare rock to the summit of Hardknott Pass. The fort at Hardknott, described below, lies just to the north of the present road, which approximates to the Roman line on the descent into Eskdale. Either the valley road or, even more pleasantly, the old packhorse route on the opposite bank of the river can now be followed to Boot, Eskdale Green and eventually the Esk estuary at Ravenglass, site of the fort of Glannaventa.

The other Roman roads in the area were all peripheral to the Lake District: in the south-east no road seems to have penetrated further than the fort at Watercrook, near Kendal, and although a road ran south-west through Greystoke from the fort at Old Penrith it apparently got no further than the low earthworks near Troutbeck which appear to represent two small marching camps. From Papcastle, near Cockermouth, another road was constructed south-east, in the direction of Keswick, and there might have been a link road from Watercrook to Ambleside, but little is known of these.

The Roman forts in the Lake District, at Ambleside, Hardknott and Ravenglass, were probably constructed shortly after the arrival of the Romans, towards the end of the first century AD, and may well have been built of turf and timber at first, before being reconstructed in stone. None of them was large enough, at least initially, to hold an auxiliary regiment, or cohort, of 500 men, and indeed Hardknott may have been properly garrisoned only fleetingly before being virtually abandoned as it became clear that there was no local threat to the Romans. The remains of all three forts are certainly worth exploring.

The fort of Galava, near Ambleside, lies at the head of Windermere and is easily recognisable as a rectangular platform raised above the surrounding meadows. The lake and the River Rothay defended the south and west, and on the other two sides ditches were added to strengthen the defences. The first fort on the site, constructed of turf and timber, was too low-lying and suffered from flooding, and during Hadrian's reign it was replaced by a stone-built fort on slightly higher ground. This appears to have been occupied until the fourth century. What is left now is the platform it occupied and traces of the foundations of the walls and main buildings.

To the west of Galava, across the Wrynose and Hardknott passes, are the remarkably impressive and dramatically situated remains of the Hardknott fort. This fort, Mediobogdum, covered about three acres and appears to have been started in 117AD, with construction taking up to twenty years. It was built to the standard Roman plan, with a tower at the four corners of a square walled enclosure and a gateway in the centre of each wall. As a result the northern gate faces out directly onto a steep drop into Eskdale and clearly serves little or no purpose; but the commandant had no authority to vary the plan to suit local conditions. The walls, well restored by the Department of the Environment, are of roughly-hewn local stone except for the gateways, which were constructed from red sandstone brought ten miles or so from Gosforth. Outside the fort to the south is the bath-house, with three principal rooms (cold plunge, warm bath and hot bath) and a furnace, while to the north-east is the parade ground, three acres of smooth and level ground improbably located in the middle of a fellside choked with tumbled boulders. But the best thing of all about the fort is its astonishing location, on a shoulder perched above the wilds of upper Eskdale and with a panorama of the more sylvan lower valley as it snakes between Harter Fell and the slopes of Scafell to Ravenglass and the Irish Sea.

At Ravenglass the field evidence for the fort of Glannaventa is somewhat scanty and visitors determined enough to seek out the earthworks are the exception rather than the rule. In fact the visible signs of the fort itself were largely destroyed during the building of the coast railway. However, to the north of the fort and its associated and apparently quite important civil settlement is a much more significant find, namely the remains of the fort's bath-house, popularly known as Walls Castle. This is the tallest surviving Roman building in the whole of northern England, with sections of the walls standing to a height of ten or twelve feet, yet it has suffered badly from abandonment and decay, so that its survival is all the more remarkable. The condition of the walls and of the pinkish internal rendering is in places excellent, and the main features of the building, including doorways, windows and little niches in the walls, can easily be distinguished. So too can the plan, with four rooms – a changing room, an anteroom and the baths themselves. At one time the remains were assumed to be those of a Roman villa, and previous legends, all lacking real evidence, variously suggested that it was a leper hospital or that it functioned as the manor house of the Penningtons before they took up residence at the nearby Muncaster Castle, or even that it was the castle of Eveling or Avallach, the Celtic lord of the underworld.

Dark Age Landscapes

Despite some pioneering recent work, it is still the case that all too little is known about the human geography of the Lake District in the years after the withdrawal of the Romans towards the end of the fourth century AD. It seems very likely that the Romano-British settlements attached to forts such as Brocavum, near Penrith, continued in existence, and that the late Iron Age settlements described previously, which had survived under the watchful eye of the legions, also survived in the uncertain times after their demise. The site at Threlkeld Knotts, for example, was probably occupied until the eighth or ninth century. By then the ancient settlement on its exposed bench on the slopes of Clough Head, with its wonderful outlook across the Glenderamackin valley to Blencathra, had outlived its usefulness; north-facing, at too high an elevation, on waterlogged ground and surrounded by poor soils, it may have been abandoned at the time of the Norse settlement, for the surviving settlements in the area, lower down in the valley and on south-facing slopes, are Threlkeld and Scales, both with placenames which are Scandinavian in origin.

After the Romans left it is likely that the British or Celtic nature of the region was reasserted, although the evidence for this is indirect, with placename evidence the only firm source. The word 'Cumberland', for example, is derived from the Celtic *cymru*, meaning 'fellow-countrymen'; the word is still in use as the Welsh term for

Wales. Other British placenames which have survived include Blencathra (*blaen* means 'summit'), Penrith and Penruddock (*pen* meaning 'head'), and Glencoyne (*glyn* meaning 'valley'). Most of the placenames with Celtic elements are clustered on the fringes of the mountains, suggesting that there was little permanent settlement in the heads of the dales at this time, and Celtic church dedications support this theory. Those dedicated to the sixth-century St Kentigern (also known, particularly in Scotland, as St Mungo), for example, lie on the edges of the northern fells, as at Caldbeck and Mungrisdale, or in the wide bowl which now houses the town of Keswick, whose mother church at Great Crosthwaite is also dedicated to St Kentigern.

Although knowledge of the Anglo-Saxon settlement of Cumbria is also largely confined to interpretation of placenames, there is in this case a little evidence that is more tangible in nature. The placenames include Brigham near Keswick and Helton and Bampton to the south-west of Penrith, though the overall distribution suggests that the Anglian settlers confined themselves mainly to the lowland edges of the Lake District, settling the Eden valley, the Kendal and Low Furness areas and the west Cumbrian coast. This impression is reinforced by the distribution of the scanty Anglian artefacts which have survived. The most notable of these is the Irton Cross, a splendid late Anglian piece of work which adorns the churchyard at Irton, itself an Anglian placename but now possessed only of a plain nineteenth-century church isolated from any settlement, though one which is blessed with a splendid distant prospect of the beckoning Wasdale and Eskdale Fells. The cross itself is a simple and quite slender slab of local red sandstone, intricately decorated with plaits and chequers and with scrolling on the narrower sides. Towards the eastern fringe of the Lake District, at Dacre, there are some fragments of the foundations of Anglian monastic buildings in and around the present church.

By the third quarter of the ninth century the Kingdom of Northumbria, which at that time included the Lake District, was under the control of yet another new group of settlers. The influence of the Norse invaders is very clearly seen in the placenames of the mountain heart of the area: elements such as *thwaite*, denoting a clearing, are common in the dales, and the frequency with which the visitor encounters Scandinavian terms such as *fell, beck, force* (waterfall) and *dale* itself is indicative of the strength of the Norse colonisation in the dales and on the fellsides. The greatest consequence for the landscape, and one which is still clearly visible, was the inexorable process of clearance which the Norse settlers instituted in the remoter daleheads, which

The Anglian cross in the churchyard at Irton

had until then survived largely unscathed. At Wasdale Head, for example, the flat flood plain of the Lingmell Beck was cleared of the boulders which were liberally scattered there; the Norsemen expended considerable energy in piling them up at random – the massive heaps are still there to be seen – and incorporated them in oversized field walls. Woodland and scrub suffered, too, as wholesale clearance and agricultural improvement took place.

Happily the most interesting of the physical remnants of the Norse colonisation is relatively accessible. This is the strange, flat-topped mound, its steep sides terraced into a series of steps, which lies behind Fell Foot Farm in Little Langdale. Informed opinion has it that this is a 'thing-mount', the meeting place of the Viking council of the Langdales – though the possibility that the mound is simply a natural phenomenon cannot quite be ruled out. More certain indications of Norse culture are the surviving Viking crosses and 'hogback' tombstones (intricately shaped and sculpted, these were the characteristic tombstones of the Norsemen, their shape representing contemporary Viking homes). The place to find examples of both is Gosforth, where there are two hogback tombstones together with a fragment of a Norse cross inside the church, and a magnificent tall, slender cross in the churchyard. Nearly fifteen feet in height, this sandstone cross has elaborate carvings which portray the triumph of good over evil in both Norse and Christian traditions. The base of the cross represents Yggdrasil, the mythological ash tree which was the foundation on which the entire Norse world was based. The remains of over twenty early crosses have been identified in the district, together with hogback tombstones at Lowther, near Penrith, and in six other Cumbrian locations.

Although the overall contribution of the Dark Ages to the present landscape is easily under-estimated, the landscape itself was subtly fashioned during these mysterious centuries, with effects which are readily apparent to the visitor today. The Norse settlement of the ninth and tenth centuries brought into existence the dalehead hamlets such as the two Seathwaites, in Borrowdale and Dunnerdale, and enhanced the bare, treeless nature of the fellsides which Wordsworth regarded as 'natural' but which are clearly the work of successive colonists from prehistoric times onwards. Before them the Anglian wave had produced a ring of villages around the mountain core but had largely left undisturbed the human geography of the dales. Here the Celts made their greatest landscape contribution, based on the creation of scattered settlements where even the church was isolated from the farmsteads it served.

The Medieval Landscape

The intensity of the struggle which the Normans faced, over a period of at least two hundred years, to establish themselves in Cumbria is marked by the series of great castles which they built in the region in order to consolidate their hold and drive back the Scots. Castles such as Cockermouth, Penrith, Appleby and especially Kendal and Carlisle were at the centre of this struggle, which saw the Scots briefly in control as far south as Morecambe Bay in the middle of the twelfth century; as late as 1172 a further Scots invasion of northern England had some initial success, but it was short-lived. From the thirteenth century onwards the invaders were restricted to brief border raids of brutal severity but only local significance.

Within the mountain core there were no such struggles and therefore no great castles. Domesday Book has little to say about the district, covering only the Kendal and Furness areas, and throughout the early medieval period the mountainous core appears to have been largely neglected. The pattern of Norman church building echoes this, for although some sixty Cumbrian churches show evidence of Norman work they are almost all peripheral to the fell country. As with their Anglo-Saxon forebears, the Normans clearly settled the fertile lowlands and were less interested in the higher ground. Nevertheless, there was some penetration into the eastern periphery of the Lake District, and both Barton and Dacre churches, in the low rolling fell country close to Ullswater, betray their Norman origins (though Dacre, at least, was a rebuilding of an earlier Anglian church).

The Normans were content for the most part to leave the economic development of the mountain resource in the hands of the monks. Although only two abbeys were sited in the National Park – Shap Abbey in a lonely valley in the remote eastern fringes, and Calder Abbey in the far west – a number of much more powerful foundations lay just outside the Park and, through their development of the large tracts of land gifted to them in the dales and on the fellsides, played a very significant role in changing the characteristics of the landscape in the medieval period. Amongst these major landowners Furness Abbey was pre-eminent.

Furness Abbey, founded in 1127, received with its charter from Stephen much of the Furness peninsula and the fells between Windermere and Coniston Water (High Furness), and in succeeding years added greatly to its land holdings in the Lake District. The most important acquisitions were the greater part of Borrowdale, bought from Alice de Rumeli in 1209 for £156 13s 4d, and 14,000 acres in upper Eskdale, acquired in 1242. This latter acquisition was that of the sheep farm of Brotherilkeld, probably first established by the Norse settlers in the tenth century, and still in existence – the long, low whitewashed farmhouse now on the site dates from the great seventeenth-century rebuilding but is redolent of the site's antiquity – as part of the National Trust's estate in Eskdale. Amongst the landscape features associated with the monks of Furness in Eskdale are the delightful packhorse bridge and sheepfold at Throstle Garth, not far upstream from Brotherilkeld and reached by a quite superb riverside footpath, and the remains of a boundary dating from 1284 which divided deer park and sheep pasture in Great Moss, the strange, flat wilderness nestling below Esk Buttress and the Scafell range.

The imprint of the Cistercian monks from Furness is strongest, however, in High Furness, an intimately picturesque area of low wooded hills and secret country lanes lying to the west of Windermere. Here the map indicates the location of the abbey's outlying sheep farms, which include the distinctively Norman placename element *park*. Examples are Park-a-Moor, situated above the woods at the southern end of Coniston Water, and, near the foot of Windermere, High Stott Park and Low Stott Park, which appear to have originated as stock-rearing enterprises. Some of these farms were so distant from the abbey that granges or manor farms were created as centres from which the far-flung estates could be managed; just outside Hawkshead the monks' grange and courthouse survives as an attractive slate and sandstone building now cared for by the National Trust. In Borrowdale the name of the hamlet of Grange-in-Borrowdale betrays the existence of another key farm.

The buildings of Shap Abbey, nestled in a shallow valley on the eastern edge of the Lake District, come as quite a surprise in bleak and largely uninhabited moorland country. The substantial tower of the abbey church, modelled on the tower at Fountains Abbey and ironically completed only just before the dissolution of the monasteries in 1536, is the most imposing surviving remnant, though there is much earlier work in the chancel. The abbey had substantial estates in the eastern Lake District, where the name of Bampton Grange gives a clue to a former monastic farm, and in the Yorkshire Dales.

On the other hand, Calder Abbey, in its secluded setting in the remote west, was less well provided for, and the monks were much troubled by Scots raiders, so much so that in 1138 the monks (only twelve in number) were driven away. Nevertheless, records indicate that the abbey later played its part in the medieval clearance of forests

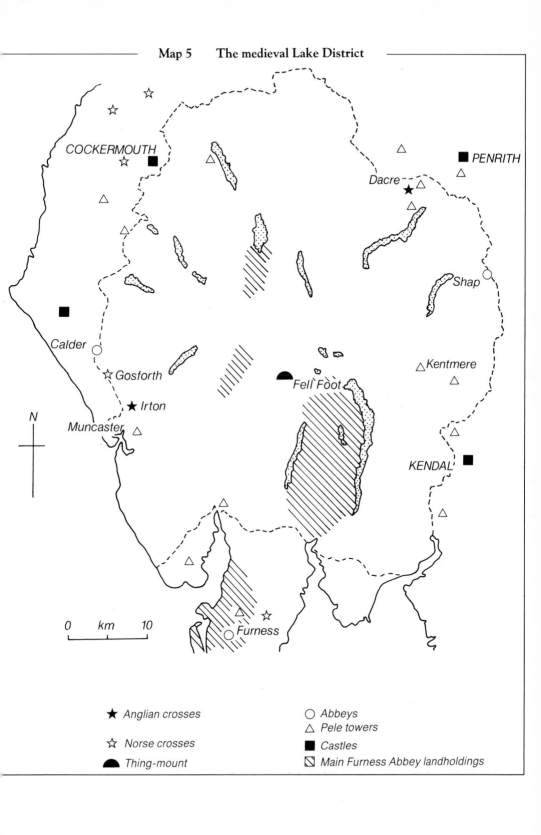

Map 5   The medieval Lake District

COCKERMOUTH

PENRITH

Dacre

Shap

Calder

Gosforth

Irton

Kentmere

Muncaster

KENDAL

N

Fell Foot

Furness

0   km   10

★ Anglian crosses   ○ Abbeys
                           △ Pele towers
☆ Norse crosses   ■ Castles
◗ Thing-mount   ▨ Main Furness Abbey landholdings

Calder Abbey

to make way for pasture. By the middle of the thirteenth century the monks were allowed to 'cut down and prostrate the branches of trees throughout all the woods of Copeland Forest, for the feeding of animals in winter'. Amongst the features to seek out are the ruins of the abbey itself, with the tower still standing to half its original height, and five bays of the west aisle remaining, together with part of the chancel; the medieval packhorse bridge (Matty Benn's Bridge), confidently attributed to the monks, higher up the valley of the Calder; and the monks' road between the abbey and Calder Bridge.

Where the monks failed to penetrate, the medieval landscape of the Lake District was one of 'forest' – either royal forest such as that of Inglewood, which included much of the fell country at the Back o' Skidda' or private forests such as Copeland, covering the western fells, and Millom, which included much of Dunnerdale. These were forests in the legal sense and were by no means all tree-covered; they were areas where forest law applied in order to preserve game for the huntsman. Within the forests clearance for agricultural purposes was illegal, though this by no means stopped it from taking place: to give just one example, names such as Harry Place, Ellers and Middlefell Place commemorate a whole series of medieval clearances in Great Langdale. By the fourteenth century this process of colonisation and creation of huge upland sheepwalks was accepted and smaller, enclosed deer parks were created for the huntsmen. Deer parks such as those at Troutbeck and in the Rydal Beck valley (an enjoyable afternoon can be spent tracing the wall built in 1277 to delineate this latter park on the slopes of Nab Scar) flourished for a while, but the rise of sheep rearing was inexorable and only a few fragments of these deer parks remain.

The prosperous early medieval period saw the growth of many settlements into villages and the creation of new market towns. Places such as Grasmere and Ambleside, originally mere outlying hamlets in much larger parishes (in this case Kendal), became chapelries and were eventually granted full parochial status. Indeed, by the fourteenth century Grasmere had 17 tenements and 7 cottages, as well as a fulling mill, a water mill, a fishery, a brewhouse and a forge. 200 years later there were no less than eighteen fulling mills harnessing the waters of the Rothay and its tributaries. The increasing population of the dales was instrumental in leading to the provision of new chapels in the comparatively remote daleheads: the church of Borrowdale, close to the hamlet of Stonethwaite, dates from this early medieval period, though the present building is entirely nineteenth century in appearance, and the older of the two chapels in Martindale dates from the thirteenth century.

By no means all of these medieval chapels, the product of a period of considerable prosperity, have survived, and the same can be said of some of the communities which they served. One such chapel was established at Boredale Hause, at the head of the remote valley of Boredale, east of Patterdale, to serve the tiny and now vanished community of Boredalehead. It is an astonishing location for such a chapel, far above the limits of present-day settlement and with the remains of the Chapel in the Hause barely discernible amongst the maze of paths which meet here. Wordsworth waxed lyrical: 'Scarcely did the Druids, when they fled to these fastnesses, perform their rites in any situation more exposed to disturbance from the elements . . . What dismal storms must have often drowned the voice of the preacher!' If the storms can be avoided, this is an especially pleasant place to visit, with fine views into the eastern fells and across Patterdale to Helvellyn. The remains of the medieval settlement of Rannerdale, on the western side of the Lake District, exist in similarly melancholy circumstances today as a result of the seventeenth- or eighteenth-century desertion of the hamlet. Slight mounds and hollows in the shadows below the steep flanks of Grasmoor now mark the site of the medieval farmsteads and the chapel of the Blessed Mary Magdalene.

The history of the Lake District's market towns displays a similar pattern of successful growth and abject failure. Most of the successful towns, however, lie on the fringes of the Lake District, with many of them – Kendal, Penrith and Cockermouth, for example – situated just outside the National Park itself. Within the Park's boundaries the resort towns of Keswick and Ambleside and smaller centres such as Coniston and Hawkshead, which are to all intents and purposes merely large villages, are the largest settlements.

Mention has been made earlier of the Scots border raids of the Middle Ages. These too have left their mark on the present-day landscape of the Lake District, not only in placenames such as Scot Rake, the slanting path on the line of the Romans' High Street as it descends into the Trout Beck valley, but also in the pele towers, defensive structures which were thrown up to provide some protection against the surprisingly severe Scots raids. These cross-border raids, at their height in the fourteenth century, had a devastating local effect. Indiscriminate slaughter, looting, and the burning of churches, houses and other buildings is recorded, and in 1322 the desperate abbot of Furness was forced to pay a ransom to secure immunity.

Pele towers, the earliest dating from the middle of the fourteenth century, were built to the simplest of plans; essentially they are bulky three-storey stone towers with very limited access on the ground-floor level; often this level was used purely for sheltering livestock. The first floor, reached via a spiral staircase, housed the main living quarters including the 'hall', while the second floor or 'bower' was the private domain of the ladies. Almost a hundred examples survive in Cumbria, with a number in the Lake District proper. Survivals in or immediately adjacent to the National Park include those at Kentmere and Burneside, in the south-east; Yanwath, Dacre, and Dalemain, all near Penrith; and Muncaster, near Ravenglass. Often the pele now forms only part of a much larger complex, notably at Muncaster, where the Castle is essentially a Victorian country house with a genuine pele and matching second tower of nineteenth-century vintage. At Yanwath the pele tower, built in 1323 by John de Sutton and including a massive tunnel-vaulted ground floor and well-preserved sandstone battlements, has a fifteenth-century hall, kitchen and courtyard attached. The superbly situated pele at Kentmere Hall, nestling beneath the Garburn Pass road and the craggy lower slopes of Yoke, is now attached to a somewhat later farmhouse. An exception to the rule, however, is provided by Dacre, well worth seeing as a fine example of a free-standing pele tower, solid and impressively battlemented.

5
TRADITIONAL INDUSTRIES AND THE LANDSCAPE

The natural wealth of the Lake District landscape has been exploited for thousands of years: rocks, fells, woodland and water have all been used to develop a series of rural and industrial economies. The mineral wealth of the area was probably first tapped by the Romans, though it was not until the sixteenth century that its exploitation was organised on a more commercial basis. A little later the great rebuilding in stone which took place in Northern England vastly increased the demand for stone as a building material, and led to the appearance of quarries, many of them small, long disused and assimilated into the landscape but some of them bigger, longer-lasting and with a much greater effect on the present-day landscape. The Lake District's woodland resources were by now in equally great demand as the basis of a flourishing iron industry in High Furness and a series of related commercial enterprises. Lakeland sheep provided the raw material for the district's woollen industry, while water power had been harnessed to provide energy for a considerable number and variety of mills. All these industries have left a distinctive imprint on the landscape, ranging from the blatantly obvious to the more subtle: these latter instances, requiring a little detective work to tease out the history of an area, are perhaps the most interesting of all.

Minerals and Mines

The extraordinary geological history of the Lake District has left the area a rich and varied legacy of mineral wealth. Possibly the first workings were those of the Romans, who appear to have smelted iron ore at bloomeries – primitive open hearths – associated with forts such as Hardknott. In medieval times the monks of Furness Abbey were equally industrious in smelting iron ore at bloomeries scattered around their extensive landholdings. But the most important Lakeland minerals were lead and copper, first seriously exploited by the Society for the Mines Royal, established under royal patronage in 1561 and using German mining expertise to develop a series of mines in the Newlands valley and, a little later, the Coniston area. A third mining area, around Caldbeck, was also founded on copper but became just as important for other minerals such as barytes (used in paper making and paints) together with zinc, iron pyrites and manganese. Other rarer minerals were locally important, including graphite (also described as plumbago or black lead), which was mined at Seathwaite in Borrowdale and formed the basis for the Keswick pencil industry, still in existence but no longer reliant on local sources of graphite. Also worthy of mention are haematite, a red iron ore which has been mined in Eskdale and the west Cumberland plain, and wolfram (tungsten), intermittently mined over the past hundred years at the Carrock mine in the lonely Caldew valley.

The Eskdale venture is particularly interesting to visitors because it has left the legacy of the Ravenglass & Eskdale narrow-gauge railway, a considerable tourist attraction. The Nab Gill iron ore mine, on the fellside above the hamlet of Boot, was first opened in the 1870s by the Whitehaven Mining Company. The ore was reached by driving an adit into the fellside, and it was transported to the coast along a 3ft gauge mineral railway. Early expansion was rapid, and the mineral line was extended across the valley to the Ghyll Foss mine, but after the collapse of the mining company in 1877 this section fell into disuse. Production continued at Nab Gill until 1912, but the mineral railway was converted to 15in gauge in 1915 and brought back into use as a passenger line, a function which, happily, it still performs today.

Whilst it is impossible to do full justice here to the many and varied mineral ventures of the past four centuries, four classic examples will be sufficient to illustrate the development and decline of the industry, its imprint on the present-day landscape, and its considerable attractions (with due care) for present-day visitors: the Newlands valley, the

Map 6   Major mines and quarries

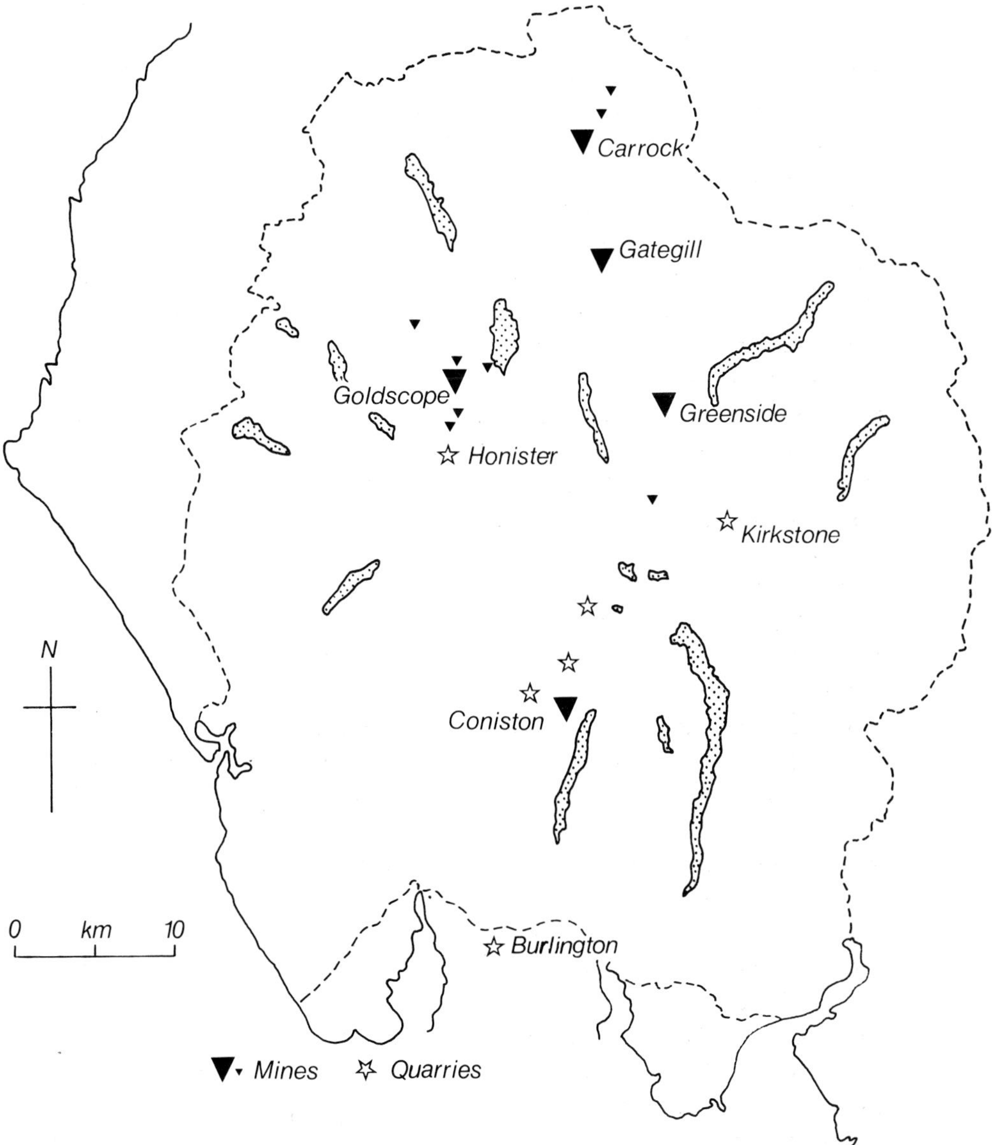

▼ Carrock

▼ Gategill

▼ Greenside

Goldscope ▼

☆ Honister

☆ Kirkstone

☆

☆ Coniston ▼

☆

N

0   km   10

☆ Burlington

▼· Mines   ☆ Quarries

Greenside Mine on the eastern flanks of Helvellyn, the Carrock Mine at the Back o' Skidda' together with the Gategill mine near Threlkeld, and the mines of the Coniston area.

Mining was in progress in Newlands by the thirteenth century, at which time a very rich vein of copper nine feet thick was already being worked at the Goldscope mine. Goldscope, which at this time was also producing lead, small quantities of silver and even a little gold, had its heyday somewhat later, however, following the importation of the German miners in the later sixteenth century specifically to exploit the Newlands mines. A period of decline later set in, and although the mine was reopened to some effect in 1847 – within a decade it was producing 300 tons of lead a year – it was finally closed down in the 1860s. Now the site is best identified from the spoil heaps which still litter the slopes of Scope End above the Newlands Beck.

Although Goldscope was the best-known of the Newlands mines, it was by no means the only substantial venture. At the head of the valley, within easy reach of the direct path to Dale Head, which itself boasts a marvellous summit panorama, the ruined sheds of the Dale Head copper mines still stand in the shadow of Gable Crag; first worked by the Germans in the sixteenth century, the mine later came into the possession of the Duke of Somerset, who built a bloomery on the site to process the ore. Amongst the spoil heaps stones with bright green veins of copper malachite can still be picked up. And at Stonycroft, below Causey Pike, a large lead smelter was built to cater for the Newlands ores; just to the north, too, the remains of the Uzzicar lead and copper mine can still be identified, though the 60ft waterwheel which distinguished the site is no longer there.

The surroundings of the Greenside lead mine, nestling in the valley of the Glenridding Beck on the eastern side of the Helvellyn massif, still proclaim that this was the most important mine of its type in the Lake District. For the industrial archaeologist the remains, which are spread over quite an area, are fascinating, not least because some of the inter-relationships between the surviving remnants are not immediately obvious. The mine buildings, alongside Glenridding Beck, have been renovated (one by the YHA) but the spoil heaps are still evident despite efforts to disguise them. Further up the valley are the remains of chimneys associated with a mile-long stone flue which was in use when the ore was smelted on the spot (later it was carted across Sticks Pass to Brigham for smelting, and later still it was sent by rail from Troutbeck station to Newcastle). Even higher there are more spoil heaps and also the site of a crushing mill below the marshy hollow which used to house

Keppelcove Tarn, converted into a reservoir for the lead mine but drained when it burst its banks after heavy rain in October 1927.

These, then, are the many and various visible reminders of a venture which began in 1822 with the formation of the Greenside Mining Company. The early success of the company was astounding, so much so that its shares increased tenfold in value in the first decade. As much as £400,000 profit seems to have been made from the quarter of a million tons of lead concentrate raised at the mine. Output in the early years of the twentieth century reached 3,000 tons a year, and the best equipment available was installed, enabling ever deeper levels to be exploited. The deposits were finally worked out, however, and the mine closed for good in 1962.

The Carrock mine, above the Grainsgill Beck in the heart of Back o' Skidda' country, is one of the most interesting to visit. It is also a comparatively recent venture, having been started in 1854 when tungsten ore was discovered in quartz veins within the Skiddaw Granite there. Early exploitation was not particularly rewarding, since tungsten had little or no value until its use as a hardener of steel was recognised. In the days of the Carrock Mining Syndicate, which was extracting tungsten ores (wolfram and scheelite) during World War I, the mine made a significant contribution to the war effort, but mining ceased when the price of tungsten collapsed in 1919. Activity has been sporadic ever since, though the mine has been periodically reopened, notably during World War II. More than twenty minerals have been identified in the immediate vicinity of the mine, and it is this which draws amateur geologists and others to the cluster of mine buildings and spoil heaps, which form an unusual feature in the open, uninhabited Skiddaw Forest grasslands.

Elsewhere in the northern fells, the ruins of the Gategill lead mine can still be seen near the village of Threlkeld. They survive as a reminder of the brief period of late nineteenth-century prosperity which transformed the hitherto sleepy village into a frontier mining settlement. The Gategill mine, together with the adjacent Woodend mine, was producing 500 tons a year of galena and a slightly greater quantity of zinc in the 1880s and 1890s. The backbreaking 'stope and feather' method of extracting the ore, named after the iron implements which were used to shatter the country rock and expose the ore, survived longer here than in other ventures, but was eventually replaced by blasting with gunpowder. Now the derelict buildings, close to the kennels of the Blencathra foxhounds, add interest to the early stages of what many consider to be the best route to the top of

Blencathra, via Hall's Fell and Narrow Edge.

At Coniston the remains of the famous copper mines are easily visited. The way lies alongside Church Beck as it rises above the village, then across Miner's Bridge and along the rough track into Coppermines Valley. Ahead is a scene of some devastation but considerable interest to industrial archaeologists. To the right is a row of former miners' cottages; ahead are the main mine buildings, now used as a youth hostel, with the stony track leading up past a multitude of mine workings clearly visible as it makes for Levers Water (and, eventually, the main ridge of the Coniston Fells). The mining of copper ores began in the second half of the sixteenth century, but it was not until 1758, when the Macclesfield Copper Company took over the lease of the mines, that the most intensive period of exploitation began.

At first the copper ore was carried by packhorse all the way to Brigham, near Keswick, to be smelted, but later it was shipped down Coniston Water to the ports of Greenodd or Ulverston to be transported to Wales. Later still, the further option of rail transport was provided when the Foxfield to Coniston branch line was opened in 1859, but by now copper mining in Coniston was in decline and most of the better deposits had been worked out. Employment in the mines, which had reached 900 at times in the 1830s, when three hundred tons a week were being produced, contracted dramatically, and by the end of the 1880s it had all but ceased. The landscape of Coppermines Valley still indicates the awesome scale of the mining activity, with huge spoil heaps, the remains of settling tanks, and the rusting wheel of the crushing plant still visible, together with mine entrances higher up the fellside towards Levers Water, a natural corrie lake but one whose level was artificially raised to serve the mines. Coniston, in fact, is perhaps the most interesting of all the mineral-working centres, largely because there has been little 20th century disruption of the main workings: a half-day spent in Coppermines Valley offers rich rewards.

Slate Quarrying

Quarrying is the largest single employer in the National Park – though tourism is not far behind, of course – with more than one in ten employed in the industry. Slate accounts for the majority of the workforce and output, but it should not be forgotten that there are also granite quarries at Shap and Threlkeld, supplying roadstone, and a series of limestone quarries around the edge of the National Park.

Workable slates are contained in both the Borrowdale Volcanics and the sedimentary rocks of the Silurian series, though ironically the Skiddaw Slates are too friable to be commercially useful. The quality of the slate varies with the area of origin, as does its colour – which varies from the attractive green of the Tilberthwaite and Honister quarries, located amongst the volcanic rocks, to the blue-grey shades more characteristic of the Silurian slates from Broughton Moor and the southern Lake District. The peak of quarrying activity was probably reached in the third quarter of the nineteenth century, and quarry closures have been common since then (even since World War II some 25 quarries have shut down) but there are still six working slate quarries within or adjacent to the National Park and demand for their products is steadily increasing. These six surviving quarries are located at Kirkby Moor, in the south-west; Coniston and Tilberthwaite; Langdale; Honister; and Kirkstone.

Lake District slate first gained widespread popularity as a roofing material in the seventeenth century, when there was a general rebuilding in stone of houses which had hitherto been constructed of less durable materials and roofed with thatch or turf. Nevertheless, there is some evidence that it was in demand for particular purposes well before this date – the barrack block at the Roman fort of Hardknott appears to have been roofed with local slate, as does the fort of Galava, near Ambleside, and some of the grander houses in the region used slate from the twelfth century onwards. The result is that the dales are peppered with small quarries which satisfied mainly local needs over a period of some centuries and which are now disused and overgrown, sometimes merging imperceptibly into the landscape and providing useful wildlife habitats, but occasionally intruding rather more into otherwise gentle scenes despite long periods of disuse. The quarries on the northern face of Wetherlam, together with their associated tip-heaps, are an example of this latter category.

By no means all of the quarries remained small-scale in their operation, however, particularly when the superior qualities of the roofing slates they produced came to the attention of architects such as Wren, who by the late seventeenth century was using them widely in London – as at Kensington Palace. The demand was for easily workable fissile slates, usually found where the rocks had been subject to intense deformation. One of the earliest major sources of supply was Honister; indeed the Honister quarries, familiar to all those travelling between Borrowdale and Buttermere, have been in continuous production since at least 1643.

Storm clouds over the widespread spoil heaps of the Burlington Slate Quarry, disfiguring the higher slopes of Kirkby Moor above Grizebeck

In the early years of production at Honister one of the consequences was a new and particularly hazardous way of life for those employed as quarrymen. The best green slate was inconveniently located towards the top of Honister Crag (still worth seeing as a dramatic piece of rock scenery, despite the effects of centuries of quarrying). At first the slate had to be crammed into sledges and manoeuvred at considerable speed down the steep fellside to Honister Pass. Originally the slate was then transported along Moses' Trod, still a spectacular high-level route across the head of Ennerdale and the scree-laden slopes of Great Gable, to Wasdale and eventually the sea at Drigg, near Ravenglass, but after the ports of Workington and Whitehaven came to prominence it was carted along Buttermere instead.

In the 1880s the sledges were replaced by gravitational railways running on inclined planes; now these are, in turn, disused and the slate is brought down to the splitting sheds by lorries which travel down from the exposed quarry face by an intricate zigzag route. The workings are undoubtedly impressive in terms of their sheer scale and the audacity associated with their operation, but the scars of past and present quarrying are all too plain and form a notable contrast with the extremely attractive local environment.

The largest slate quarry in England is the Burlington quarry on Kirkby Moor, the successor of the tiny quarries hacked out by the farmers on Gawthwaite Moor in the eighteenth century, as they slowly realised that quarrying was more profitable than farming. By 1810 more than 25,000 tons of 'Westmorland Dark Blue' slates (so-called despite the fact that they were produced in Lancashire) were being won every year from the Kirkby quarries and ferried down to ports such as Greenodd, which enjoyed a brief prosperity based on slate while, as was reported in 1818, 'several sloops are constantly employed in the carriage of it to almost every principal seaport town in England and Ireland'.

The Woodland Industries

Within the National Park there are a number of fascinating and easily accessible sites which between them reveal a good deal of the history of the woodland industries in the Lake District. They illustrate, too, one of the pressures which dramatically reduced the woodland cover of the area in medieval times – the other major factor being agricultural clearance for sheep farming.

The source of this pressure was the burgeoning medieval iron industry of Furness, which required vast quantities of charcoal in order to smelt the iron ore. So great was the demand for charcoal – and hence so extensive was the area of woodland used – that the monks of Furness Abbey, who were the prime movers in this industrialisation, established their smelting hearths, or bloomeries, in the woods of High Furness rather than next to the iron ore deposits in the Dalton area of Low Furness. The bloomeries were concentrated in the Coniston area and the Rusland and Leven valleys; a good example is the site (its name an evocative giveaway) at Cinder Hill on the wooded slopes of the Leven valley above Newby Bridge.

The monks of Fountains Abbey were equally prepared to establish their bloomeries close to the source of charcoal: their woodland resources in Borrowdale were exploited using a bloomery established in the unlikely location of Smithymire Island, a tiny island at the junction of Greenup Gill and Langstrath Beck. It is hard to believe that this delightful spot, with its foaming, cascading waters and miniature gorges, was the place where iron ore from around Ore Gap, on the 800m (2,600ft) contour between Bowfell and Esk Pike, was brought for

The scanty remains of the Backbarrow iron works, first opened in 1711 but now represented only by a sorry series of dilapidated buildings alongside the River Leven

smelting before being carted along Borrowdale for distribution.

These early, primitive and inefficient methods of charcoal-burning and smelting proved inadequate to meet demands in the sixteenth and seventeenth centuries, especially when the Society for the Mines Royal widened its sphere of operations to include the Coniston area. Pitsteads, or charcoal hearths, were built in many Lakeland valleys – not just in Coniston but around Ullswater and in the upper Troutbeck valley running up towards Kirkstone Pass. The Forestry Commission's Grizedale Forest trails include examples of these pitsteads, though the last charcoal burn took place somewhat further south, at Ealing Hearth near Backbarrow in 1936. A more widespread and more picturesque reminder of the charcoal workings is the delightful coppice woodland of the low fells between Coniston Water and Lake Windermere; coppicing, in which oak, hazel and ash were cut across the base every 12 to 15 years, was designed to promote rapid growth to meet an almost insatiable demand for timber.

Iron smelting in the fells was gradually concentrated at larger and more sophisticated smelters, the first of which was built at Cunsey, on the western shores of Lake Windermere. A bloomery was operating here by 1623, but less than a century later a smelting furnace had been built by ironmasters from Cheshire; now the water leat and the heaps of iron slag are the only obvious remains. Other eighteenth-century furnace sites were those at Backbarrow (the largest of all, founded in 1711 and working continuously until 1965), Low Bridge, Penny Bridge and Nibthwaite, together with Spark Bridge and Force Forge, two names which emphasise the former importance of the iron industry in the area. At Nibthwaite, close to the River Crake, the forge oven and the site of the forge survive, but the mill itself is a later rebuilding.

As the nineteenth century progressed the iron industry declined and much of the southern Lake District's remaining woodland was pressed into service as the raw material for a variety of smaller and more intimate craft industries. These included the manufacture of pit props, pick and hammer shafts, brush handles, swill baskets and barrels, though by far the most important of these industries was bobbin manufacture, which developed to service the textile industries in

The bobbin mill at Low Stott Park, closed in 1971 but happily restored as a working museum

This chimney at Bobbin Mill Bridge near Ulpha in Dunnerdale is the only tangible reminder in the dale of the industry, which sustained 64 mills in the nineteenth century

Yorkshire and Lancashire. Of the 25 bobbin mills which were in production at the beginning of the twentieth century, only two survived the 1960s, largely because of competition from Scandinavia and, more recently, the replacement of wood by plastic. The bobbin mill at Caldbeck, wrecked by fire and long since disused, can still be seen in its remarkably constricted position in the deeply-etched limestone gorge known as The Howk; it once boasted a waterwheel 13m (42ft) in diameter, reputedly the largest of its kind in England. The five mills around Staveley, on the River Kent, have gradually closed, though wood turning and paper making survives there. The last outpost of the bobbin industry was located much further west, at Spark Bridge on the River Crake; its final competitor was the mill at Low Stott Park, at the foot of Lake Windermere, which latterly employed only a handful of workers and finally closed in 1971, but happily has been restored as a working museum, with much of the machinery still in place.

The coppice woodlands, and specifically those of ash, had yet another use, that of providing charcoal for gunpowder manufacture. The first mill was built in 1764 by John Wakefield at Sedgwick, south of Kendal and just outside the National Park, but ash charcoal from High Furness was soon being used in gunpowder mills at Low Wood, Gatebeck, Blackbeck and at Elterwater in Langdale. Much of the gunpowder produced in these works was used locally, in the slate quarries and copper mines of the Coniston and Keswick areas, though some was exported as far afield as Derbyshire. The industry died out in the 1920s with the introduction of new explosives such as dynamite, and the closure of Low Wood in 1936 saw the end of another rural Lake District industry. At Low Wood the buildings, including an imposing tower, can still be seen, but at Elterwater the greatest surviving contribution to the landscape is probably the much-visited corrie lake of Stickle Tarn, which was dammed and raised in level to provide an adequate source of water power for the gunpowder works some distance downstream.

The imposing tower of the former gunpowder works at Low Wood near Haverthwaite which closed in 1936

Woollens and Water Mills

The lakes and in particular the rivers of the Lake District have been a considerable natural asset to the development of its rural economy, not least with the provision of water power for some of the developments discussed in the last section. Originally, however, the rivers and streams were harnessed for corn mills and, in the later medieval period, the fulling mills which – using the fleeces of the hardy sheep which now thickly populated the fellsides – formed the cornerstone of a once-flourishing local woollen industry.

Although its natural centre was Kendal, just outside the National Park, the manufacture of the cloth was really a cottage industry. The wool was collected, carded, spun and woven on Lakeland farms – hence the spinning galleries, which are discussed further in the next chapter – and then taken to one of the many fulling mills which had been established by the sixteenth century. In Grasmere parish alone there were eighteen mills at this time; sadly none of them have survived. The decline and fall of these scattered mills was brought about by the invention of more sophisticated machinery, which in turn needed the power provided by mills on the main rivers. The Kent valley, which was also well placed for exporting the finished products to the rest of the country, became pre-eminent.

Other areas fared less well. The hamlet of Millbeck, nestling under the slopes of Skiddaw to the north of Keswick was, as its name suggests, highly dependent on its mills for its livelihood. New fulling and carding mills were built in the early nineteenth century to produce a variety of materials – blanket checks, flannel, kersey and even carpets. But competition from the larger and better located Yorkshire mills, combined with falling demand, led to the closure of the mills in 1886; the carding mill survives as a private house. At Caldbeck, where the woollen mill (downstream from the bobbin mill already described) specialised in producing a heavy grey overcoat cloth known as Ivenson Grey, the work lasted rather longer but has long since ceased, leaving yet another abandoned mill to excite the curiosity of tourists drawn to the village by its associations with John Peel.

Not all the disused woollen mills found a new purpose and a new lease of life, then, but quite often the best sites were adapted to new uses and remained in production for centuries. The industries concerned ranged from corn milling through woollens and cotton – there were cotton mills in the southern Lake District, at Backbarrow (the Dolly Blue works) and Spark Bridge, in the eighteenth and early

The Dolly Blue works at Backbarrow, once a cotton mill but now ingeniously converted into an hotel and timeshare complex

nineteenth centuries – to tanning, brewing, saw milling and iron manufacture. Villages such as Caldbeck and hamlets such as Millbeck, as we have already seen, were heavily dependent on the employment generated by the mills, but it is not always appreciated just how many settlements were in this position: for example Lorton, now a quiet village in the delightful Buttermere valley, developed entirely because of its attractions for water-powered industry. Jennings Brewery, a rare example of a surviving independent brewery, has been located in Cockermouth since 1887, but originated in Lorton in 1828 and moved only when demand for the beer outstripped the capacity of its premises in the village.

Ambleside owes its early growth to the suitability of Stock Ghyll, a fast-flowing stream in a steep-sided woodland gorge, as a source of water power. At least half a dozen mills – corn mills, fulling mills, bark mills, a bobbin mill and a paper mill – were established here. The former corn mill on the north bank of the stream has been restored quite recently; it originally dates from the fourteenth century, and by 1639 was in the hands of the Braithwaite family of Ambleside Hall. Corn was still being ground here until early in the twentieth century, but it is now a pottery and shop, and the overshot waterwheel, with a diameter of 5m (16ft), is a reproduction dating from 1973. Although the water mills no longer support a local woollen industry, knitwear is still produced for tourists by Ambleside firms.

Two mills within the National Park have been carefully restored and opened to visitors. At Boot in Eskdale the former corn mill by the Whillan Beck, constructed of the local pink granite, is the successor to the manorial mill which was in operation by the thirteenth century. The present mill was operating until the 1920s and includes an excellent example of a drying loft, where the corn was dried over tiles before being ground. There is also a working waterwheel. Cumbria County Council began the restoration of the mill in 1975, and a decade's painstaking work has certainly brought its rewards. The Whillan Beck also supported a carding mill, and the ruins of this – the highest building in the valley – can still be picked out above Gill Bank Farm.

Still in Eskdale but closer to the Irish Sea coast is Muncaster Mill, restored to working order by the Eskdale (Cumbria) Trust in the 1970s. There was a mill on this site by 1470, though the present structure is only about 200 years old. Corn was milled until 1914, then oatmeal and cattle feed for the next forty years until it was closed down in 1954. Now the mill, which boasts a 4m (13ft) overshot waterwheel, produces oatmeal and wholemeal flour, and visitors are able to observe the whole operation, from kilning the oats through husking, sieving and grinding to the production of the finished article.

6

THE BUILT LANDSCAPE

The contribution of man to the medieval landscape was discussed in Chapter 4, which reflected on the Norman colonisation of the Lake District, the very substantial influence of the monks on the area, and the response of the area's inhabitants to the threat posed by the cattle raiders from across the Scottish border during the turbulent early Middle Ages. That response was often to construct pele towers, solid defensive structures for use in times of strife. In more peaceful times non-fortified extensions offering greater comfort though less security could be contemplated. But these peles were rarities in the landscape, which until at least 1600 contained few stone buildings; medieval farmhouses were generally less solidly built and none, sadly, has survived. Building in stone did, however, become commonplace from the seventeenth century onwards, and it is to this period that we now turn, considering the form of these new dwellings and seeking out some of the best surviving examples. The contribution of the stone walls of the Lake District to the present-day landscape is also explored.

Just as important to the understanding of the present landscape, however, is a grasp of the factors which caused certain of the settlements in the district to take the first steps along the road to their present status as towns. Some of these settlements failed, despite the ambitions of their promoters, to make much progress and lapsed into sleepy villages which these days contain only a few hints as to their former importance: Ireby, Hesket Newmarket and Ravenglass all fall into this category. Keswick, Ambleside and Kendal, amongst others, successfully achieved urban status – as, later and for different reasons, did Windermere – in ways which are explored in the second part of this chapter.

Change in the Countryside

Except for a number of the dale churches and the fortified pele towers described in Chapter 4 there was little or no building in stone before the early part of the seventeenth century. The most important reason for this would seem to be the general poverty of the area in medieval times. The farmhouses of the period before about 1650 were simple structures of clay and timber; they were not built to last and therefore there are no surviving examples for us to see. An excavated example from the Lune valley, outside the National Park to the south-east, indicates the general style, with a wooden cruck frame, walls of dried mud plastered over a thin timber framework and signs of a roughly thatched roof. Domestic building in stone before 1600, where it did occur, concerned only the upper echelon of medieval society and even then was confined to the southern Lake District and in particular High Furness, comparatively unscathed by the Scots raids which prompted the building of pele towers in more vulnerable spots. Amongst the few examples of these early non-fortified dwellings are Coniston Hall, cruck-framed and with cylindrical chimneys, Hawkshead Old Hall and Graythwaite Hall.

Increasing prosperity in the seventeenth century, allied to the emergence of the rural middle class yeomen farmers known as 'statesmen', led to the great rebuilding in stone of many of the farmhouses and (somewhat later) cottages of the district, in an authentically regional style which still embellishes many a dale. The statesmen were essentially tenant farmers who had acquired the right to hereditary tenure by signing up for military service in the troubled border regions; their wealth was based on a smallholding together with the right to graze the extensive fell pastures. The building style was based on the concept of a long, low building which included farmhouse, byre and store all in one. Originally the human and bovine quarters were separated merely by a narrow passage, and the entire construction was single storey, with the bower or sleeping quarters beyond the kitchen. Such a house plan showed few changes from its prehistoric and Dark Age forerunners. From the early eighteenth century onwards, however, an upstairs bedroom approached via a staircase in a projecting wing became more common.

The exterior of these statesman farmhouses, whilst it conforms to a general pattern, also varies with the underlying geology to such an extent that variations in rock type are immediately apparent in the visual impact of the farmhouses on the landscape. The overall pattern, however, remains that of a low building of extreme length, usually externally roughcast or whitewashed, and with a slate roof which, in the case of the earlier examples, is probably the successor to a heavy stone-flagged roof which needed the support of fairly massive roof timbers. Stone flags were increasingly relegated to use for floors only from the mid-eighteenth century onwards, and within a hundred years flagged floors were becoming less common. Local variations derived from geological differences – because almost without exception these farmhouses were constructed from stone won from very local quarries – include the roughly worked, angular blocks from the Borrowdale Volcanics in the central core of the district, the sandstones of the Penrith area, more amenable to the mason's touch, and the light grey carboniferous limestone of the Kendal and Ulverston areas and also of the northern fringe, notably in Hesket Newmarket, Caldbeck and the surrounding hamlets.

A classic example of a statesman farmhouse formed from the angular rocks of the mountain core is that at Dalehead, in its remote location at the limit of human settlement in Martindale. Long, low, roughcast and with the date 1666, indicating the date of rebuilding, inscribed on one of the stone buttresses which once supported a spinning gallery, Dalehead is a worthwhile though difficult detour for visitors to Ullswater. Somewhat more accessible is the unique collection of statesman farmhouses in the village of Troutbeck, not far from the tourist honeypots of Windermere and Ambleside. There are over a dozen farmhouses dating from the seventeenth century, and though some have more recently suffered dereliction or have been altered significantly, the majority retain their original plan and their sense of place.

By far the best known of the Troutbeck farmhouses is the former home of the Browne family, Town End, now cared for by the National Trust. Built in 1623, Town End not only has the classic external attributes of the statesman farmhouse, including in this case the tall cylindrical chimneys characteristic of Westmorland, but has also retained period furnishings, including pieces of furniture carved by members of the Browne family. Across the road is Town End's barn, a bank barn of a type restricted to the Lake District and the Yorkshire Dales, two-storey and with a ramped entrance to the hay store on the upper floor. A gallery connected the two floors and this has been described as a spinning gallery, though this may not have been its purpose at the time it was constructed.

Spinning galleries, of which mention has already been made on more than one occasion, are found in a number of locations in the Lake District, including the Coniston area (Yew Tree Farm on the road to Ambleside), Cartmel Fell (Pool Bank Farm and Hodge Hill), Troutbeck, and Low Hartsop in the upper Patterdale valley. They constitute an impressive and historically important link with the domestic woollen industry which was so significant a part of the rural economy in the seventeenth and eighteenth centuries. The purpose of the galleries was to provide a covered area for the drying of Herdwick fleeces and for the subsequent spinning of the fleeces into wool which could then be taken to the fulling mills of the district. The importance of the spinning galleries was that they increased the potential income of the statesmen at a time when the smallholdings, small enough to begin with, were being further subdivided through the system of hereditary tenure into parcels of land which were barely sufficient to support farming families.

Town End at Troutbeck, the best known of the seventeenth-century statesmen's houses in the Lake District

Mireside, Hartsop – a classic Lakeland farmhouse, with exterior staircase and an unimproved spinning gallery

Once widespread in the district, spinning galleries are now a rarity, but one which is well worth seeing. The best, perhaps, are those at Hartsop, which illustrate the range of sophistication which was achieved in their design, from the comparatively simple, roughly shaped stone structure at Mireside to the superficially more attractive wooden balcony, with its reminders of the black-and-white architecture more common further south, at Thorn House. The spinning galleries here, and their parent slate farmsteads below the green slopes of the eastern fells, probably date from about 1700, though it is difficult to date individual examples too closely.

By 1790 the *Gentleman's Magazine* was able to conclude that in the Lake counties 'the houses (or rather huts) of clay, which were small and ill-built, are mostly thrown down; instead of which, strong and roomy farmhouses are built'. Yet whilst this was true of the middle-class farming community, the rural lower classes existed for the most part in less comfortable conditions until the late eighteenth and early nineteenth centuries, when the rebuilding of cottages – and considerable building of new artisans' dwellings – was prompted by increased demand for labour in the quarries, mines, and mills, which were still in many cases prosperous. These cottages often replaced less durable predecessors constructed of clay and wood, and were usually constructed of solid, thick walls of limewashed rubble or slate blocks, with small windows and doors set deeply into the walls as one source of protection against the winter weather.

The great age of rebuilding still has a dramatic impact on the landscape of the dales, where the whitewashed statesman farmhouses stand out amongst the valley pastures yet harmonise with the patterns of field and fellside, and on the more urban landscape of the villages and hamlets, where the vernacular architecture of farms and cottages is an important cohesive element in the scene. Yet there is a much more widespread legacy of the eighteenth and nineteenth centuries in the landscape of the fells and dales, namely the drystone walling which was a consequence of the enclosure movement. The enclosure walls account for the majority of the stone walls which survive on the fells, though more ancient boundaries – including those of monastic estates and medieval deer parks – can also be traced in places.

The enclosure of the Cumbrian commons largely took place between 1760 and 1800, with some 50,000 acres enclosed during that period. The process was easily achieved on paper but rather more difficult to put into practice because of the mountain topography. Walls, often still in good condition, traverse many of the high fells, running along the summit ridges and often then plunging down fellsides along lines defined more on the map than in the landscape. A good example is the wall which comes steeply up from Martindale onto the southern flanks of Wether Hill on the High Street ridge, runs south along the ridge almost as far as the top of High Raise and then veers dramatically westward down a savagely eroded rocky ravine into the Rampsgill Beck valley.

These walls, which Hugh Walpole described as 'running like live things about the fells', were built by wallers who would often camp out on the fells for several days at a time, painstakingly constructing the walls with their hogg-holes to let the sheep through, their large stones or 'throughs' projecting on both sides to stabilise the wall, and their 'cams', stones laid vertically on top of the wall at its normal height of 4ft 6in. The cost was eight shillings for 6m (7 yards) of wall in 1845. Despite the standard method of walling which was employed, regional characteristics persisted, largely as a result of differences in the raw material, from the rounded pinkish boulders of Eskdale granite through the friable grey slabs of the limestones to the massive angular blocks of the Borrowdale Volcanics. Whatever the rock, the result is a highly significant contribution to the attractiveness of the landscape.

The Growth of Towns

There is no evidence for the existence of towns in and around the Lake District until well after the Norman conquest, although it is clear from the sites of several that there were pre-existing settlements of some sort in the area – Roman forts and associated civil settlements at Penrith and Kendal, for example, and an early Dark Age village close to Keswick. The impetus for urban development came from the establishment of markets and fairs, and indeed a great rash of market charters punctuates the twelfth and thirteenth centuries. The layout of many of these towns reflects their former importance as market centres: Penrith has a whole series of open market places. Keswick, too, is built around a widened main street which functioned as the market place during its period of rapid expansion in the late medieval period.

The development of these towns can readily be appreciated on a walk around their medieval cores, particularly since the buildings which survive, constructed of local stone in most cases, have a very distinctive personality and character. Penrith, for example, exudes the confidence of a successful medieval market town with the solidity of its red sandstone, a solidity much needed in facing up to the Scots border raiders to whom it was peculiarly vulnerable. Kendal, its buildings derived from the local grey limestone, and Hawkshead and Coniston – the latter two, constructed largely from the dark Silurian slates, are really large villages with some pretension to town status – are other examples of the importance of locally available building materials in setting the style of a town.

The development of the major towns in the National Park, and those on the fringes which play an important role for Park residents and visitors alike, is sketched below, with further notes in the Gazetteer on these towns and the other important settlements such as Hawkshead. But it is also worth considering the settlements which attempted the transition between village and market centre in the medieval period, but which failed to achieve it. There are a surprising number of them, and an exploration of the reasons for their failure also throws some light on the reasons for success of the main towns, perhaps better located, or with access to crucial raw materials or to water power, or backed by more powerful vested interests, or simply favoured by luck.

Perhaps the most interesting of these failed market towns is Hesket Newmarket, now a delightful large village on the north-eastern fringes of the Lake District. The name itself betrays the pretensions of the place, and the layout of the village, with cottages dispersed around a wide green, is similarly revealing. The market cross is still there, too, though the markets and fairs ceased by about the middle of the nine-teenth century. Not far away, Ireby still has a Moot Hall, butter cross and spacious market place to serve as reminders of its former status, which can be traced back to the grant of a Thursday market and annual fair in 1237. Market charters also existed at places as diverse, and nowadays as quiet, as Bootle, Flookburgh and Staveley, and at Shap, where the charter dates from as recently as 1687.

A final example of a settlement which tried without success to achieve urban status in the Middle Ages is Ravenglass, which is not only well worth exploring on account of its attempted medieval expansion but which also, as the site of a Roman fort and port, has a history unrivalled amongst this clutch of failed towns. Ravenglass was granted its first market charter in 1209, and for some time the Saturday markets and annual fair were highly successful, especially while the town also functioned as a port and trade with Ireland was substantial. Towards the end of the seventeenth century decline set in, however, and the three-day fair petered out; an attempt by Lord Muncaster to breathe new life into the place by obtaining a new charter in 1796 for two markets a week and three annual fairs met with success for only a short while and now the annual fair is merely a tourist attraction.

Ambleside

Though it has been a market centre since the seventeenth century and has more recently become highly important as a tourist centre, Ambleside has a longer history than this, having originated in medieval times as a small settlement at the edge of Grasmere parish. Its origins were modest, with nothing more than a few farmhouses and a chapel in the area known as Above Stock, well above the flood plain of the River Rothay. This is still the most pleasant part of Ambleside, away from the tourists and the traffic and with steep, narrow streets leading up to How Head (partly constructed with stones from the Roman fort of Galava and with an interior still with sixteenth-century

The medieval Court House at Hawkshead, originally the grange farm of the monks of Furness Abbey

features) and St Anne's Hall, the former church.

The early growth of Ambleside owed much to the fast-flowing waters of Stock Ghyll, which were pressed into service to power at least half a dozen mills, including a bobbin mill, a corn mill, fulling mills, bark mills and a paper mill. The former corn mill on the north bank of the beck has been restored recently and has a reproduction overshot waterwheel; the mill originated in the fourteenth century, was in the hands of the Braithwaite family by 1639, and was still being used to grind corn in the early years of this century. A little further upstream a former bobbin mill has been converted into holiday flats.

Ambleside was granted its market charter relatively late, in 1650, when the Countess of Pembroke was granted a charter to hold a Wednesday market. The market place, with its cluster of inns and shops, is still the focal point of the town, though the sheep have long gone and been replaced by tourists. Many of the nearby cottages date from the eighteenth century, when Ambleside had a considerable reputation for its wool sales. By 1800, however, the market was in decline and the town was saved only by the growth of another industry, that of tourism. Close to Windermere and with very easy access to the central fells – in particular Langdale – Ambleside was popular with rich manufacturers in the nineteenth century and their villas spread out around the town, at the head of Windermere and towards Waterhead, where there is a steamer service on the lake. Today Ambleside has a strongly Victorian flavour, but caters almost exclusively for tourists and is almost overrun with gift shops and guest houses.

Cockermouth

As with many settlements in the Middle Ages, Cockermouth grew into a town with the construction of a castle and the subsequent grant of a market charter, in this case to William de Fortibus in 1221. The castle was built in about 1140, partly with stones robbed from the nearby Roman fort of Derventio at Papcastle, and the town grew in its shadow at the confluence of the Derwent and Cocker. Its early growth was slow and it was not until the seventeenth century that the weekly horse and cattle fairs spawned a physical expansion of the town, with blue-slated town houses built of stone around the Moot Hall, Market House, Corn Market and Shambles. Industrialisation followed in about 1800 and resulted in growth north of the River Derwent, around Derwent Mills, and also south of the medieval centre, close to corn, tweed, hat and fulling mills.

This early nineteenth-century expansion transformed Cockermouth from a small market town into a busy industrial centre (though still on a comparatively small scale) and its legacy is very much to be seen in the character of the town today. The Cockermouth commons, known as The Sand, were enclosed in 1816 and replaced with workshops and warehouses between Main Street and the River Derwent, and the lasting visual impression of the town is of the Georgian and early Victorian buildings which accompanied this development. Examples include the Town Hall, dating from 1841 and first used as a Methodist chapel, and, from a slightly earlier period, the house on Main Street which has achieved fame as William Wordsworth's birthplace.

Kendal

Though it is just outside the National Park Kendal acts as a centre for much of the south-eastern quadrant; it was formerly the biggest town in Westmorland. Sited close to the Roman fort at Watercrook, Kendal achieved urban status under the Normans, with a busy town stretching out along roads such as Stricklandgate, Stramongate and Kirkgate from its central market place. The first market charter – the first granted to any Lakeland town – was granted by Richard I to Gilbert fitz Robert fitz Reinfred in 1189 and bestowed the right to hold a Saturday market and three fairs a year in the barony of Kendal. The massive circular motte and bailey castle, perched on top of a drumlin to the east of the River Kent, dates from the early thirteenth century; three centuries later it was already in decay, and the remains of towers and the curtain wall are a little disappointing.

The medieval prosperity of Kendal was based on wool from the surrounding fells, not just brought to market here but woven into the heavy cloth known as Kendal Green; Flemish weavers settled here from the fourteenth century onwards. The long, narrow 'burgage' plots of the weavers and the other burgesses of the medieval town can still be traced running in both directions from the main north-south streets, while at the end of alleys leading from these streets the traditional style of buildings clustered around yards can still be found. Though this was also medieval in origin (and timber-framed houses from this period still exist, some disguised by the application of rendering) most of the surviving houses in this style date from the great expansion of the late eighteenth and early nineteenth centuries.

This expansion followed the construction of the Lancaster and Kendal canal, which opened in 1819, and resulted in the creation of an industrial suburb on the east bank of the Kent, immediately below the ruined castle. The new industries, largely using water power from the river, included carpet-making, the manufacture of railway rugs and coat linings, snuff manufacture, and marble polishing. Terraces of cottages, built in the local grey limestone, also appeared in the early nineteenth century close to Stramongate bridge, together with St George's church in 1841, though the parish church remains Holy Trinity in Kirkgate.

Keswick

The original focus of settlement at Keswick was at Great Crosthwaite, some distance to the west of the present town but still the site of a pleasantly rural church. This was, indeed, the mother church of the vast parish of Borrowdale; it is dedicated to St Kentigern, an early evangelist who was reputedly the builder of the first church on the site in 533AD. As late as 1306 Crosthwaite market was supplying 'corn, flour, beans, peas, linen and cloth, fish and flesh' on Sundays, while Keswick was little more than the 'dairy farm' indicated by its placename.

A number of factors contributed to the rise of Keswick in medieval times, notably the energy of the Derwentwater family in obtaining a market charter and its role as a centre for the mining enterprises in Borrowdale and the Newlands valley; ores from the mines here were smelted at Brigham, in the Greta valley just upstream from the town centre. The discovery of plumbago (also called wadd, black lead and graphite) on the fellside above Seathwaite in Borrowdale encouraged further growth with the opening of the world's first pencil factory at Keswick in 1566. The Cumberland Pencil Factory is the modern successor to that first enterprise, though for some considerable time now its supplies of graphite have been imported.

In the late medieval period Keswick was in some difficulties, for the mining industry had entered a period of recession in about 1650, and the woollen industry – at its height in the sixteenth century, when complete hamlets such as Millbeck were dependent on it – was also in retreat, with mills closing or turning to cotton. The town was described as 'greatly decayed and much inferior to what it was formerly' in 1749. Tourism arrived in the nick of time, growing even more rapidly after the arrival of the railway in 1864, so that 'Lakes Specials' were running between London Euston and Keswick by 1900. Though the railway is no longer there the hotels and guest houses survive, indicators of the importance of tourism to the town today.

Penrith

Although Penrith, like Kendal and Cockermouth, lies outside the National Park, it is one of its main market centres. As with the others it was sited close to a Roman fort – in this case Brocavum (Brougham) a little distance to the south. Henry III established a market at Penrith in 1123, though it had been in existence as a settlement providing services for north-south travellers for some time before this. The churchyard gives some clues to this earlier phase of the town's existence, for it contains Viking hogback tombstones and some slightly battered sandstone crosses which also pre-date the Normans.

The grant of the market charter led to considerable growth, particularly since Penrith had the status of a royal manor after Richard III's accession and was the centre of the Honour of Penrith – a territory which included much of Inglewood Forest and the Eden valley. It is still possible to walk around the town and recognise from its layout the main elements of its medieval success, in particular the succession of open spaces which formed specialised market places. These include Sandgate, Burrowgate, Market Square, Corn Market and Great Dockray. Whilst Market Square saw trade in a variety of goods such as woollens, meat, poultry, eggs and butter, the huge, irregular space at Great Dockray was the site of the important Penrith cattle fairs, and Sandgate was the home of the weekly stock market as well as of the cruel sport of bull-baiting until it was suppressed in the early nineteenth century.

Penrith's position astride the main route from Scotland to the south, together with its medieval importance as a trade centre, made it an easy and also an important target for the Scots border raiders, and it suffered accordingly. The town was sacked in 1314, after Bannockburn, burned by 'Black Douglas' in 1345, and burned again in 1382. The castle, which was progressively enlarged throughout the Middle Ages in response to the border raids, still stands as a massive sandstone reminder of these troubled times. In the times of peace which followed the Union, Penrith prospered again and the town had become a principal stopping point for stagecoaches by 1800; it was, however, left behind in the Industrial Revolution because it was unable to develop industries based on water power, and although the railway added a new artisans' quarter, Castletown, to the town its status declined somewhat, and it now functions mainly as a market centre for the surrounding area.

Ulverston

Whilst Ulverston has a long history and was a successful market town in the sixteenth century its major period of development came two hundred years later, when it became a busy industrial town and port – though this is by no means immediately obvious to the casual visitor today. The parish church dates from the twelfth century, but was much restored in Georgian and again in Victorian times, and the town received a market charter in 1280. It was not until the Elizabethan era, however, that it really began to prosper. Ulverston began by taking trade from Dalton-in-Furness after the dissolution of the monasteries had robbed Dalton of the important patronage of Furness Abbey (an outbreak of plague in 1631 finally sealed Dalton's fate), and continued to such good effect that it seriously affected trade at the markets of Broughton, Cartmel and Hawkshead. In 1805 Thomas West commented that the market place, by now surrounded by a variety of buildings in the attractive local limestone, was too small to accommodate all the business transacted there.

Ulverston built on this success in the late eighteenth and early nineteenth centuries, using its natural advantages of local iron ore, charcoal from nearby High Furness, and water power, and combining them with an ambitious scheme to develop the town as a port. A mile-long canal was dug to link Ulverston to the sea, and an export trade in iron ore boomed, with wharves close to the town and a 'capacious basin' busy with sea-going traffic. Other exports included slate from the quarries of southern Lakeland, cotton, canvas, sailcloth and the like from the town's mills, and local leather, gunpowder, and timber. Shipbuilding became an important employer, together with the manufacture of anchors and ships' chains. The population rose to an estimated 50,000 (more than three times the present figure).

It was, of course, too good to last. The emergence of Barrow-in-Furness hit hard, the canal began to silt up, and the Ulverston ironworks were overtaken by others using more modern and efficient processes. Now, although some new industries have come, Ulverston has reverted to its former role as a quiet country town, one which only really comes to life on Thursdays, when the boisterous and colourful market is the focus of attention. The canal, however, is still worth following from the town to the Leven estuary at Canal Foot.

Blea Water, the deepest corrie tarn in the Lake District, and High Street, its summit plateau traversed by a Roman road

Windermere

The town of Windermere grew in response to forces which were quite different from those which affected the other towns described in this chapter. Though there was settlement in the area in prehistoric times – the site at High Borrans, just above the town, may be Iron Age in date – Windermere existed merely as a hamlet called Birthwaite until 1847. The order consecrating the chapel and parochial graveyard in 1348 was not a sign of growth; in fact it was quite the opposite, since it was a direct response to the Black Death. The hamlet's elevation to urban status was a consequence of the opening of the Kendal and Windermere railway in that year, despite the ardent protests of conservationists, who almost inevitably included Wordsworth among their number. The conservationists may have been defeated here but were able to chalk up a victory somewhat later, when the plans for the extension of the railway to Ambleside were thrown out.

Birthwaite became a magnet for tourists and also for wealthy businessmen, who clamoured to build ever more ostentatious Italianate and Victorian gothic residences along the shores of Windermere lake and along the roads leading from Bowness to the former hamlet, which for commercial reasons was renamed Windermere. The pace of expansion and the lack of controls in the nineteenth century have created a sprawling form of development alien to the area, though its impact is reduced by the local topography and the well-wooded nature of the area. Many of the businessmen's houses are now hotels and guest houses; the town inevitably lacks historical interest, though it fulfils its primary function of tourist centre admirably.

Birks Bridge, a classic packhorse bridge spanning the River Duddon, here running through a miniature gorge

7

EXPLORING BY CAR

Picture the scene: waves lap gently at the rocky shore of the lake, and in the background the rugged sweep of the Coniston Fells, from the Old Man himself right round to Wetherlam, is seen in perfect proportion. Far from being an example of the peace and quiet which only a good tramp in the fells can bring, this is a description of the view confronting a motorist parked in the pleasant woodland car parks south of Brantwood on the east shore of Coniston Water. For the truth is that the Lake District is the most accessible of areas, happy to reveal most (though certainly, and quite rightly, not all) of its charms to the most casual of visitors. It is almost as if the place recognises that there are those without the ability, energy or time to explore in minute detail. So here are five motor tours to whet the appetite of those confined to car or coach.

Keswick, Borrowdale and the North-west

This is a short and straightforward route which includes the majority of Borrowdale, the awkward but highly scenic Honister Pass, delectable Buttermere and the forests around Whinlatter Pass. Leave Keswick along the B5289, passing on the left Castle Head, a volcanic outcrop which now forms a natural viewing platform of such quality that John Ruskin was moved to describe the scene, including Derwentwater and the north-western fells, as 'one of the three or four most beautiful views in Europe'. To the right is Friar's Crag, another celebrated viewpoint, and a series of little bays looking across to Lord's Island and Derwent Isle, two of the islands formed on the underwater ribs of rock which run the length of the lake. The Radcliffe family, founders of Keswick in the thirteenth century, built their manor house on Lord's Island, while Derwent Isle was the site chosen by the sixteenth-century German miners for their 'colony'.

The Borrowdale road next passes through Great Wood, the shore of Derwentwater very close but only occasionally glimpsed – the narrow road to the spectacularly pretty hamlet of Watendlath leaves to the left – and after leaving the lake behind runs below the Lodore Falls, a 12m (40ft) cascade which needs heavy recent rain to look its best, and Shepherd's Crag, where rock climbers may well be at work, to Grange-in-Borrowdale, originally the site of an outlying monastic farm but now best known for its double-arched bridge over the River Derwent. Further south the valley sides begin to press in as the Jaws of Borrowdale are approached. Ahead to the right is Castle Crag, separated from the fellside above by an ice overflow channel and colonised by hillfort builders in Romano-British times; to the left, at a much lower level, lies the remarkable sight of the Bowder Stone, a 2,000 ton boulder which is the best-known glacial erratic (a boulder transported by ice away from the site where it outcropped) in the Lake District.

The upper Borrowdale valley opens out around Rosthwaite, a pleasant hamlet sited on a little rocky platform. The flat valley floor here was the site of a former lake and is still subject to occasional flooding. To the left is a charming view along the side valley containing Stonethwaite, with the rocky bastion of Eagle Crag dominating the scene. The road along Borrowdale continues to the right, however, to the hamlet of Seatoller, originally the Norsemen's 'summer dwelling by the alder tree' but growing somewhat later with the construction of quarrymen's cottages as Honister quarries expanded. A lane here leads further into the head of Borrowdale, ending at Seathwaite, notorious as the wettest place in England and the starting point for the vastly popular walkers' route over Sty Head to Wasdale or to Scafell Pike, but the main road now begins to climb steeply up Little Gatesgarthdale to the Honister Pass, its summit a scene of some devastation with slate waste and old quarry buildings. Nevertheless this is the site of historic and visually impressive slate quarries and also offers the chance to take in mountain scenery of some distinction.

The mountain scene improves still further on the descent from Honister into the Buttermere valley; here the road is hemmed in between the flanks of Fleetwith Pike and Dale Head, but there are magnificent views ahead of the High Stile ridge beyond the still waters of Buttermere. It is worth stopping at Gatesgarth Farm to survey the scene, from the end-on view of Fleetwith Pike's main ridge through the depths of Warnscale Bottom and the rugged, complex outline of Haystacks, a favourite fell of many, to the High Stile ridge itself. The ridge encompasses three mountains: High Crag, attacked by many via the Scarth Gap Pass and the rivers of scree around Gamlin End, but much more rewarding when tackled from Birkness Comb, a fine corrie basin ringed by crags; High Stile, highest of the three and with a wonderful prospect of the Grasmoor fells; and Red Pike, perched above Bleaberry Tarn and easily picked out from the red screes on its flanks. The north-eastern side of the valley is less exciting, with the lower slopes of Robinson, a mountain of great bulk but little finesse, blocking out the view.

At the far end of the lake the village of Buttermere, with its inns and ice cream, caters almost exclusively for visitors, though there is a tiny dale chapel, a post office and a cluster of farms. The alluvial flats beyond the village were once under water, but deposition of material from Sail Beck and Sour Milk Gill has separated Buttermere from Crummock Water, whose highest reaches are now some distance below the village but are quickly brought into view. Opposite Hause Point the track up to Floutern Tarn and Scale Force, at 50m (170ft) the biggest waterfall in the district, can be picked out, while Rannerdale Farm, a little further along the road, is a reminder of the former hamlet of Rannerdale, which had its own chapel in medieval times but was deserted by the eighteenth century. By the time the parking area at Lanthwaite Green is reached the impressively steep western slopes of Grasmoor focus the attention; there is a direct way up Grasmoor End from here, but it is backbreaking work and most of those who stop here will keep to the level paths among the bracken on Lanthwaite Green itself.

The route is reasonably clear as far as the village of Lorton – two settlements really, High and Low, which were formerly dependent on water mills sited on the River Cocker and its tributaries. Turn right to go through High Lorton onto the B5292, which climbs steadily to reach the summit of Whinlatter Pass. Near Scaw Gill there is an excellent view of the conical summit of Grisedale Pike and, connecting it to the equally shapely Hopegill Head, the crumbling cliff of Hobcarton Crag, treacherously steep and fragile but an important haven for plant life. Even here the conifers have encroached on the lower slopes, and the road soon plunges into the Forestry Commission's

The view from the fell gate at the delightful hamlet of Mungrisdale, with the valley of the Bullfell Beck separating the smooth slopes of The Tongue and Bowscale Fell

Thornthwaite Forest, not so gloomy now that felling has commenced but still forming a green blanket snuffing out the views. At the top of the pass a visitor centre dispenses information and mugs of tea and is the focus for several forest trails. On the descent to the workaday village of Braithwaite the views suddenly open out, with Skiddaw very prominent across Bassenthwaite Lake. The end of the tour is now close at hand, with two right turns to be made, onto the A66 past Portinscale and then onto the B5289 into Keswick.

Keswick and the Northern Fells

This is essentially a tour of the gentle Skiddaw Slate country, taking in Skiddaw and Blencathra and also the Caldbeck and Uldale Fells, together with a string of attractive and fascinating villages. Start by taking the A591 out of Keswick, then turn left onto the old Penrith road and immediately right along a lane signposted to Castlerigg stone circle. It is well worth stopping here not only to see the ancient stones but also to savour the panorama, including the bulk of Skiddaw, the serrated southern face of Blencathra, the north-western ramparts of the

Helvellyn range and, across the Derwentwater basin, the summits of the Grasmoor group.

Return to the Penrith road (A66), which bypasses Threlkeld and Scales, two Norse settlements nestling at the foot of Blencathra, but turn left onto a minor road leading to the pleasant little village of Mungrisdale. The road now runs right at the base of the fells and as the hamlet of Bowscale is reached there is a delightful view of Carrock Fell, its summit crowned by one of the Lake District's few hillforts, to the left, and the low hills running down to the Eden valley to the right. On the way to Mosedale the road crosses the River Caldew; slightly further downstream is the attractively arched predecessor to the present bridge. Next is the large village of Hesket Newmarket, once a would-be market town and still with its market cross and enormous village green as reminders of the sheep and cattle fairs which died out in the nineteenth century.

Caldbeck, a large straggling village which is perhaps less self-conscious about its image than those knowing of its John Peel associations would expect, is the next destination. This was very much an industrial centre, with a quite large woollen mill close to the village centre and a bobbin mill – destroyed by fire – tucked away in the eerily atmospheric limestone gorge known as The Howk. West of Caldbeck the views open out markedly and there are fine opportunities for the landscape photographer, with the northern sentinels of the Lake District all clearly visible. The road eventually swings round towards Ireby, another former market town which is a shadow of its former self, though here there is still a market square and Moot Hall to serve as a reminder of former times. Some distance to the west is the old church of Ireby, a largely Norman chapel which has long been disused. The farming hamlets of Ruthwaite and Orthwaite are next to be visited; close by here is Over Water, a low-level tarn in an area showing evidence of its glacial past, and to the south-east there is a tremendous view into Skiddaw Forest, that lonely and unfrequented moorland which provides a quiet Bank Holiday haven for walkers trying to escape the crowds.

Follow the minor road as it twists and turns around the moorland edge before reaching Bassenthwaite, a considerable village but some distance from Bassenthwaite Lake. It is also quite a way from the present village to Bassenthwaite old church, along a narrow lane close to the lake. The way back to Keswick now runs along the western flanks of Skiddaw, the summit of which is hidden behind outliers such as Carl Side and Dodd, the latter a little wooded fell with good forest trails and

Sharrow Bay, Ullswater

an excellent prospect southwards into the heart of the Lakeland mountains from its summit plateau. Below Dodd is Mirehouse, open to the public, the former home of James Spedding, the author of *The Life and Letters of Francis Bacon*; amongst his visitors was Tennyson, whose *Idylls of the King* was inspired by the lakeside views here. A final detour under the slopes of Skiddaw takes in the hamlets of Millbeck, once an important centre of the Keswick woollen industry but now best known as the starting point of a popular route to the summit of the mountain at whose foot it shelters and, a little further south, Applethwaite.

Ullswater and the Eastern Lake District

Perhaps the best starting point for this tour is the village of Shap, conveniently located on the A6. Minor lanes lead quickly to Shap Abbey, a surprising survival in a deep wooded valley; the tower of the abbey church is particularly striking. On the way to Bampton a roadside limekiln serves as a reminder that this is Carboniferous Limestone country, while the placename of Bampton Grange indicates that the hamlet originated as an outlying farm of the nearby abbey. At Bampton, a quiet and unremarkable village, take the road to

Haweswater and Mardale Head, passing through woodland before reaching the reservoir. Haweswater assumed its present form in the 1930s to serve Manchester's needs but this necessitated the drowning of the hamlet of Mardale Green; the ghostly remains of the church, pub (the Dun Bull) and cottages can still be seen during times of drought. Here too are the first views of the magnificent array of mountains which ring the head of Haweswater.

Beyond the hotel the Old Corpse Road over Mardale Common to Swindale and Shap, once used to carry Mardale's dead but now a quiet walkers' route, leaves on the left, whilst straight ahead, above the jutting wooded promontory of The Rigg, can be seen the narrowing ridge of Rough Crag and Long Stile, the best way to the top of High Street. To its left is the deep corrie containing the unseen Blea Water, deepest of the district's tarns, and further left still is Harter Fell, its craggy northern buttresses jutting proudly between two famous packhorse routes, over Gatescarth Pass to Longsleddale and over Nan Bield Pass to Kentmere.

Return to Bampton and take the surprisingly wide road north to Helton. A very worthwhile detour to the left here leads up to Helton-head and the open common land of Moor Divock, a prehistoric hive of activity and studded with ancient survivals, including a stone circle (The Cockpit) later used as a sighting point by Roman road builders, cairn circles and standing stones. There is also a very fine prospect across Ullswater to the Helvellyn range from the common. North of Helton is Askham, an excellent example of a green village, with the Lowther Castle estate beyond the River Lowther to the right. The ruined Lowther Castle, lavishly rebuilt in the nineteenth century but now only a facade, and the curious church of St Michael standing beside the site of a medieval village deserted when the Lowthers decided to create a spectacularly landscaped park, produces scenery of an unexpected and slightly disturbing kind. At Lowther Newtown, slightly to the east, is the seventeenth-century replacement for the village.

The route now lies along a narrow lane to Celleron – where the Roman High Street is crossed – and Pooley Bridge at the foot of Ullswater. Turn left before the church here and take the equally narrow road (on which parking is subject to severe restrictions) which runs along the east side of the lake, with marvellous views of the Helvellyn foothills and the boating activity on Ullswater itself, to Howtown, where boats leave for Glenridding Pier and Pooley Bridge. The road runs on to Martindale, a delightful spot with two churches (the older one a typically simple dale chapel) and a variety of walks, from quiet treks through virtually unknown valleys such as Bannerdale and Boredale, to the very short and quite popular stroll through rocky knolls to the low summit of Hallin Fell, with the reward of further excellent views of the lake.

There is no through route for cars from Martindale, so return to Pooley Bridge and take the main road along the western side of Ullswater, perhaps pausing at one of the many parking places but certainly stopping at the medieval deer park of Gowbarrow Park, where a splendid path follows the Aira Beck upstream to that most excellent of waterfalls, Aira Force. Above the waterfall the fellside, with little crags interspersed among the bracken and fine views along Ullswater to the mountains around the head of the lake, is a place to linger, while down below the battlemented folly of Lyulf's Tower, a late eighteenth-century hunting lodge, adds further variety to the scene. The main road (A592) continues to hug the shore of the lake as far as the former mining village of Glenridding, then leaves Ullswater behind on its way to Patterdale and, along a quiet side road, Hartsop. This is a classic Lakeland hamlet of little cottages, a number of them with exterior spinning galleries, though few of the farms are still worked and most are occupied as second homes. Just beyond the village is the attractive tarn of Brothers Water, while the side valleys of Dovedale and Deepdale, each of them ending in remote coves surrounded by considerable crags, lie across the main valley as it approaches the Kirkstone Pass.

To the south of the pass, a narrow defile between scree-laden slopes, a side road runs down into the tourist trap of Ambleside, but the main road leads on towards Troutbeck, a spectacularly pretty series of linked hamlets with attractive statesman farms (the most notable of them Town End, now owned by the National Trust) and wide views across the Trout Beck valley to the green, shapely Ill Bell range of fells. Turn left onto the A591, skirt the town of Windermere and, at the mill village of Staveley, turn left again to follow a series of country lanes past the entrances to the pleasant eastern dales of Kentmere and Long-sleddale to the A6, which forms the National Park boundary for most of the return journey to Shap.

Windermere, Coniston and the Langdales

This is essentially a route to be savoured in spring or autumn, when the roads in this, the most popular of the Lake District's sub-regions, are least likely to be congested. Start in the town of Windermere, a product of the nineteenth century, its expansion the result of the arrival of the railway, the growth in tourism and the attractions of the area for northern businessmen, who soon populated the town and the shores of the lake with ornate villas and gentlemen's residences. Beyond Bowness the lake is glimpsed only occasionally through the trees and beyond the country houses, some of them now hotels, but there is a fine view across the lake from Beech Hill. Just beyond here a lane on the left gives an optional detour (on steep and very narrow roads in places) over Cartmel Fell, with the chance to visit the fine, isolated pub on Strawberry Bank, to see the spinning galleries at Hodge Hill and Pool Bank, and to find the isolated chapel of Cartmel Fell, with tremendous views over the sands of Morecambe Bay from the rocky knoll above the chapel.

Towards the southern end of Windermere it is possible to visit another, rather more accessible viewpoint – Gummer's How, reached by footpath from the lane above Fell Foot and with a splendid prospect northwards along Windermere and west across the fells and forests of High Furness towards the Coniston valley. At Newby Bridge, take the A590 alongside the River Leven to Backbarrow, with its former iron works, and Haverthwaite, terminus of a steam railway, before turning right onto a series of country lanes heading for Finsthwaite, Low Stott Park, another industrial hamlet noted particularly for its bobbin mill, and Cunsey, where a footpath leads to the early iron smelting site at Cunsey Forge. Eventually the route arrives at Far Sawrey, close to the Windermere ferry; turn left along the B5285 through Near Sawrey, a delightful hamlet sometimes overrun with tourists seeking out Hill Top, Beatrix Potter's former home, and alongside Esthwaite Water, a low-key lake in a sylvan setting, to Hawkshead. This is an attractive large village, a market centre in medieval times, with timber-framed houses, Wordsworth's grammar school next to the church and, just to the north, Hawkshead Court House, formerly a grange belonging to Furness Abbey.

Turn left, still on the B5285, just before the Court House and make for Coniston. A road on the right at Hawkshead Hill can profitably be followed since it rises slowly to arrive at Tarn Hows, that celebrated viewpoint for the Langdale Pikes and centre for gentle walks around the (man-made) tarn. Turn left again just before Coniston is reached, to follow a road which runs close to Coniston Water as far as Brantwood, for long the home of John Ruskin and now open to the public. A little further south are pleasant car parks in the woods, with a very good view across the lake to the Coniston Fells. Return to the head of the lake and turn left into Coniston, a rather plain slate-grey village but the centre for excursions to Coppermines Valley, a scene of industrial devastation but tremendous interest, to the Walna Scar Road, a prehistoric track across Little Arrow Moor to Seathwaite in Dunnerdale, and especially to the Old Man of Coniston and the rest of the Coniston Fells.

From Coniston the A593 leads north, past the entrance to the scenic Tilberthwaite valley and High Yewdale, a picturesque group of farm buildings with a fine spinning gallery, to the awkward, steep turn into the Little Langdale road. These initial difficulties are soon forgotten, however, as the view opens out and the hamlet of Little Langdale itself is reached. Leave the car here and follow a lane, then a footpath, down to Slater Bridge, a quite magnificent slate-slab bridge over the River Brathay just below Little Langdale Tarn. The bridge, made by workers at the slate quarries whose waste heaps still disfigure the slopes of nearby Wetherlam, was probably also used by Lanty Slee, a notorious whisky smuggler whose illicit stills were located on the mountain. The tarn forms the foreground in views from here of the Wrynose Pass, followed by the Romans and now by the narrow road which twists and turns on its way to Dunnerdale and, via the even trickier Hardknott Pass, to Eskdale.

An alternative to Wrynose is to take the equally narrow but less steep road on the right just before Fell Foot Farm, with its strange mound, reputedly a Scandinavian thing-mount, is reached. This gated road leads over to Great Langdale; just beyond the gate there is a car park on the right and it is worth turning in here, then strolling down to the shores of Blea Tarn, attractive in its own right and also effective as a foreground for the Langdale Pikes, which become dominant features in the landscape here. The road drops down into Great Langdale, a valley of dramatic contrasts, with the flat floor of the dale around the famous climbers' pubs such as the Old Dungeon Ghyll backed by scree and crags rising almost sheer to the summit regions of the Langdale Pikes. At the head of the dale, which here splits into two – Oxendale and Mickleden – is Bowfell, a superb mountain usually climbed by the track which starts at Stool End Farm and ascends The Band, the prominent spur dividing Oxendale from Mickleden.

At New Dungeon Ghyll, where there is a very large car park, the path ascending by the side of Mill Gill (also known, romantically but inaccurately, as Stickle Ghyll) can be taken as far as Stickle Tarn. The tarn, artificially dammed to provide a water supply for the gunpowder works in Elterwater, occupies virtually the whole of a vast bowl at the foot of the dark grey crags of Pavey Ark with, to the left, the slopes of

Harrison Stickle, the highest of the Langdale Pikes. Back in the valley, the road winds through Chapel Stile and past Elterwater, a reed-fringed lake below a pleasant common, before reaching Skelwith Bridge, near the attractive series of rapids known as Skelwith Force. The main Ambleside road now passes through Clappersgate, where Langdale slate used to be loaded onto barges and sent down Windermere, and close to the site in Borrans Field of Galava, Ambleside's Roman fort. Windermere town is now only a few minutes' drive away, past the pier at Waterhead, the fringes of Lake Windermere and the National Park Centre at Brockhole.

The Western Dales

The remoteness of the western Lake District, difficult to reach directly from the most popular centres, has protected it from the worst excesses of the tourist industry. Yet the mountain scenery is at its most magnificent here, as witness the cluster of noble fells crowding in at the head of Wasdale, and there is tremendous scope for a rewarding tour – though not a circular tour, since two of the dales have no through road, another factor in preserving them in their present largely unspoilt state.

The first dale to be explored is Ennerdale, probably the least known of all. The public road ends at Bowness Knott, and further progress up the dale has to be made on foot; few will go too far, however, because the extensive Forestry Commission plantations block out many of the views. It is probably better to climb the little rocky knoll of Bowness Knott and enjoy the wide sweeping view across the lake, from Angler's Crag up to the extensive, grassy Skiddaw Slate fells of Grike and Caw Fell, then further left to Haycock – a fine winter mountain – and Pillar, with the awesome Pillar Rock jutting out of the fellside at three-quarter height. Then follow the pleasant, quiet lanes to the sleepy village of Ennerdale Bridge and take the fell road south, past the Kinniside stone circle and the rather haphazard plantations of Ennerdale Forest to Cold Fell Gate.

Another excellent detour here lies along the track to the left, which descends steadily into the Calder valley. Cross the river on a modern footbridge next to a ford, then walk upstream for a couple of minutes to arrive at Matty Benn's Bridge, a packhorse bridge ascribed to the monks of Calder Abbey. The situation is delightful, with the clear river in a rocky gorge below the bridge, but the bridge itself is suffering from decades of neglect and the luxuriant vegetation is beginning to take over. Strong walkers will perhaps continue over Tongue How to reach

The stepping stones below Wallabarrow Crags on the River Duddon

Stockdale Moor, thickly littered with prehistoric remains (including the long cairn known as Sampson's Bratful), but this is a considerable trek in remote and rather featureless country, and it may be more prudent to return to the car and continue south to a junction of roads near Calder Abbey. The monks at this minor outpost, originally a Savignac priory, were twice raided by the Scots, but twice returned and exerted some influence in the medieval colonisation of Copeland Forest; extensive remains of the abbey survive to enhance the scene in the quiet Calder valley.

Turn left onto the main road at Calder Bridge, uncomfortably close to Sellafield, then left again to follow the Wasdale road through the large village of Gosforth, notable for its tall, slender Viking cross and hogback tombstones, to Buckbarrow and, with stupendous views opening up in front, the Wasdale valley. This is as near perfection as English mountain scenery can be: a ring of craggy mountains at the head of a long, brooding lake with the threatening Wastwater Screes apparently streaming down into the lake on the right. The ring of mountains includes Yewbarrow, Kirk Fell, the glorious Great Gable, Lingmell and the two Scafells – Scafell Pike above Pikes Crag and, to

Seathwaite Bridge, a splendid two-arched bridge over the River Duddon in upper Dunnerdale. Harter Fell forms an effective background

the right of the declivity of Hollow Stones below Mickledore, the dramatic northern face of Scafell. As the road nears Wasdale Head the interplay between these mountains and Wastwater continually changes, and at Wasdale Head itself still further mountains crowd into the scene, notably Red Pike and Pillar above the deep glacial bowl of Mosedale. The hamlet of Wasdale Head is equally full of interest, with a little dale chapel, the well-known Wasdale Head Inn, a classic packhorse bridge, and a series of easy walks among the intake fields, many of them with notably thick walls piled with the boulders which were painstakingly cleared by the Norse settlers.

Return along the dale road, this time keeping close to Wastwater all the time, to pass the youth hostel at Wasdale Hall and, just before Strands, turn left onto the Santon Bridge road. Another left turn onto the Eskdale road leads past the entrance to the little-visited Miterdale and through Eskdale Green, which has two stations on the narrow-gauge Ravenglass & Eskdale railway. Keep on the Eskdale road to Dalegarth, where there is a car park which enables motorists to stretch their legs with a stroll around Boot – highly recommended, since there is much of interest. Don't miss the little church of St Catherine, down by the river near some stepping stones; the packhorse bridge over the Whillan Beck; or the adjacent, recently restored, woollen mill. Above Boot the valley narrows and becomes less sylvan in character, with the rocky summit of Harter Fell prominent on the right and the first hints of the major peaks at the head of Eskdale, beyond the statesman farmhouse at Brotherilkeld, on the left. Leave the car near Brotherilkeld and walk up to the Roman fort of Hardknott, perched high above the Esk and a tremendous tribute to the determination of the Romans. The remains, painstakingly restored, are considerable and include the walls of the fort itself and the principal buildings, together with the bath-house some distance away to the south, and a parade ground somewhat higher up to the east. And the Scafell range, Esk Pike and Bowfell form an effective background at the head of the Esk valley.

The final dale, Dunnerdale, can be reached across Hardknott Pass, but those who are deterred by the extraordinary gradients and hairpin bends will return down Eskdale until, a little beyond Boot, a left turn can be made onto the narrow road which leads over Birker Fell to Ulpha in the Duddon valley (Dunnerdale). A track on the right can be followed to the remote tarn of Devoke Water, but attractive though this is the panorama to the left is even more dramatic, with the highest land in England seen in perfect perspective across Eskdale. Beyond Crosbythwaite the road drops steeply down into Ulpha, with its typical dale chapel. A little further up Dunnerdale is Seathwaite, a tiny hamlet but the centre of dale life. It is well worth exploring here, with stepping stones across the Duddon and the rocky buttresses of Wallabarrow Crag and Low Crag amongst the attractions. Higher still, as the dale scenery becomes more bleak and the shapely peak of Bowfell asserts itself on the horizon, the magnificent high-arched packhorse bridge of Birks Bridge crosses the Duddon, which at this point is trapped in a particularly attractive gorge, with sheer rock above deep green pools of clear water – a fitting climax to an exploration of the western dales.

8
LOW LEVEL WALKS

The vast majority of those who come to walk in the Lake District – and the appalling state of some of the main routes shows that there are many of them – aim to conquer at least some of the major peaks. But walkers who confine themselves to these popular, and often crowded, high fells, such as Helvellyn, Skiddaw and the Langdale Pikes, are robbing themselves of a wealth of interest and enjoyment. The Lake District's valleys and less exalted fells are not just the preserve of the very young and the very old, or to be regarded as worthy of exploration only on days when weather conditions put the high fells out of bounds for the majority: they have their own character and attractions.

There are, indeed, some quite outstanding walks in the dales and amongst the lower fells, often following ancient routes or using paths which offer magnificent views of the main mountain groups. In this chapter I have divided the walks into four types: those around the lakes, those which explore the dales, those which traverse the many low-level passes which connect adjacent dales, and finally a selection of those which conquer some of the lesser-known lower fells.

Stickle Tarn, a corrie tarn whose waters were harnessed for use in the Elterwater gunpowder works, and the forbidding crags of Pavey Ark. The exciting scrambling route known as Jack's Rake can be seen rising diagonally from right to left across the face of the crags

THE LAKES

Some of the best low-level walks are those which follow the shores of the major lakes (either completely around the lake or, in the case of the larger lakes, for a convenient section of the circuit); they have the dual attractions of marvellous views close at hand, sometimes linked to boating activity too, and outstanding panoramas of mountain systems hemming in the dalehead. Not all of the lakes can provide a satisfying circular tour, however. The shores of Wastwater, for example, are too close to the valley road on one side, too hemmed in by the dangerously loose, steep slopes of The Screes on the other. But the examples I have chosen, whilst they might be said to represent the cream of the available routes, by no means exhaust the possibilities for shoreline walking.

Buttermere

Amongst these lakeside walks the first to spring to mind for many people would probably be that around Buttermere, set in one of the most romantically scenic of Lakeland dales. Starting at the village, the route lies past the Fish Inn and across the flat meadows which now divide Buttermere and Crummock Water; in earlier times these meadows, too, were under water, and the two lakes were joined together as one. Below the ravine of Sour Milk Gill, recently scoured out afresh by a savage winter landslide, the lakeside path keeps to a good track which bears left through the trees, keeping a little above the lake. There are increasingly fine views of the head of the lake and the spine of Fleetwith Pike at the dalehead.

Below High Crag the old track from Wasdale Head and Ennerdale, coming down from the Scarth Gap Pass, joins in from the right, and the path now crosses the lake flats to the farm at Gatesgarth. The low-lying land here was all once part of a much larger lake. A little road walking follows now, though it is by no means dull, for there are splendid views across the lake to Haystacks, one of the most delectable of the lower fells in the Lake District, with its succession of summit tarns, and to the High Stile range. Soon the lakeside footpath can be rejoined and followed through fields which can be thick with buttercups at times to the tiny cluster of farms, cottages and hotels which makes up the popular village of Buttermere.

The spectacular view of Newlands valley and Skiddaw from the superb cairn on the summit of Dale Head

Derwentwater

A more exacting circular tour follows the shores of Derwentwater –
though perhaps it is best if two segments of the circle, along the busy
valley road from Grange to Friar's Crag, and from the landing stages
around Keswick as far as Portinscale, are omitted. The first walk, from
the landing stages south to Friar's Crag, is short but delectable, past
Cockshot Wood and along the lake shore opposite the equally well-
wooded Derwent Isle. Friar's Crag is, of course, one of the most famous
beauty spots of the Lake District, easily accessible from Keswick and
blessed with one of the best overall views of Derwentwater, with the
jutting summit ridge of Causey Pike prominent across the lake.

The second Derwentwater walk, along the western side of the lake, is
much longer, from Portinscale to Derwent Bank and then through the
gardens of Lingholm, renowned for their rhododendrons and azaleas, to
Copperheap Bay, the point from which the ore won from the mines at
Goldscope and Dale Head was once shipped across Derwentwater to
the smelter at Brigham, near Keswick. The path then runs below
Hawse End, where the popular and very easy walk along the Catbells
ridge begins, before plunging back into the woods of Brandlehow Park,
the first acquisition of the fledgling National Trust. A delightful feature
here is the profusion of little rocky bays with white shingle beaches.
The walk then passes the remains of the Brandlehow lead mine, the
largest and oldest of Borrowdale's lead mines, and skirts Manesty Park –
the island in Abbot's Bay is called Otter Island – before finally reaching
Grange-in-Borrowdale, best known for its double bridge across the
Derwent, by path and the stone-walled Field Lane. As its name
implies, the village was once the site of a monastic 'grange', built by the
monks of Furness Abbey to control their land in Borrowdale.

Ullswater

The third of the lakeside examples is the classic walk along the shores of
Ullswater from Howtown to Patterdale. For much of the way the walk
traverses the lower slopes of Place Fell, itself an attractive destination
for a short excursion, with an unparalleled view of the upper reaches of
Ullswater and the surrounding peaks. Regarded by many as the best
low-level walk in the district, the lakeside stroll is distinguished by a
series of intimate views along the upper reaches of Ullswater, from
Howtown Bay to the head of the lake, and into the craggy recesses of
the dalehead peaks, whilst itself traversing rocky country which gives

the feel of a real expedition. The journey through the woods on the lower slopes of Hallin Fell, from the boat landing at Howtown past Kailpot Crag to Sandwick is especially memorable. And the best way back to Howtown is by ferry from the landing stage at Glenridding Pier, a memorable way of reviewing the highlights of the walk which has just been completed.

Tarn Hows

Tarn Hows is the final destination in this section; not one of the major lakes at all, it is nevertheless eminently worthy of inclusion because of the very pleasant nature of the immediate scenery (best viewed out of season, for it is enormously popular despite rather haphazard signposting from some directions) and the outstanding views to some of the high fells, in particular the Helvellyn range and the Langdale Pikes. The tarn, though, is an artificial addition to the landscape, created in the nineteenth century by damming a small stream and flooding an area of swampy and low-lying ground. Nowadays it is in the care of the National Trust, and good work has been done in controlling erosion and providing pleasant lakeside paths.

THE DALES

Eskdale

Eskdale reigns supreme for low-level walks in the dales, with a remarkable selection ranging from the remote traverse of Great Moss below the towering cliffs of the Scafell range, through the sylvan delights of the mid-valley near Boot, to the easy walking over Muncaster Fell and around the Esk estuary. Perhaps the best of all is the riverside walk from St Catherine's chapel at Boot, upstream at first over rocky ground alongside the Esk, here characterised by swirling rapids, deep silent pools of delightfully clear and cold water, and tiny rocky gorges. Cross the river at Doctor Bridge, an imposing single-arched bridge carrying the farm road to Penny Hill and the path to the superb rocky summit of Harter Fell. Now turn downstream along the south bank, passing through the farmyard at Low Birker and skirting Great Coppice on the way back to the chapel – accessible across the river only by means of stepping stones which are slippery and, except in times of drought, usually awash.

Better, then, to carry on along the southern bank, passing Stanley Ghyll (possibly diverting here to the splendid waterfall higher up the

The simple dale chapel of St Catherine at Boot in Eskdale

gill, in a deep, well-wooded and steep-sided ravine) and Dalegarth Hall, the former manor house of the Stanley family, with round chimneys but no longer any vestige of the pele tower which was added in the fifteenth century. Now a lane can be followed down to and across the Esk, with a bridleway – latterly a marvellous walled green lane – leading back to the chapel on the riverside.

Dunnerdale

The next spoke anticlockwise in the Lake District's 'wheel' of valleys is Dunnerdale, probably the least spoilt of them all and certainly amongst the prettiest. There are no major mountains here, though there are distant glimpses of Bowfell and its neighbours from near the valley head and of the Coniston Fells (though not at their most photogenic) and Harter Fell from around Seathwaite. The valley walking is delectable though discontinuous; amongst the best routes are the walk from Cockley Beck to Birks Bridge, in the footsteps of the Romans as far as the solid farmstead at Black Hall, then alongside the river past the sharp little turret of Castle How and below the forestry plantations on the flanks of Harter Fell to Birks Bridge, a classic and much photographed hump-backed bridge taking nothing more grand than a rough track over a marvellous rocky gorge on the River Duddon. Lower down the Duddon valley there are excellent riverside walks around Seathwaite, a timeless hamlet which acts as a focal point for the upper valley, and lower still at Ulpha there are good walks on uncrowded paths and bridleways with fine views of the fells.

Troutbeck

Third amongst the 'dale' walks is one which hardly qualifies as such; indeed, if the place it explores were any larger it might well be classified as an urban trail. The place is Troutbeck, neatly bypassed by the busy main road from Windermere over Kirkstone Pass to Ullswater, and the attraction is a complex village landscape of intersecting lanes, clusters of farms and cottages grouped around the wells from which communal water supplies were obtained, and points of historical and architectural interest. The best-known feature of the village is the series of 'statesman' farmhouses it contains; these were the architecturally distinctive farmsteads built by the newly prosperous yeoman farmers of the seventeenth century. The classic 'statesman' farmhouse is Town End, and this is as good a place as any to start. The home of the Browne family for more than 300 years from 1623, it has miraculously survived almost unchanged, with its cylindrical Westmorland chimneys and mullioned windows and, inside, items such as an old-fashioned cheese press, wooden washing machine and antique mangle. Opposite Town End is a seventeenth-century bank barn, of a type found only in the Lakes and in the Yorkshire Dales, and as the village street straggles northwards a further dozen examples of statesman farmhouses can be spotted, though many are no longer associated with farm holdings and have become the desirable residences of offcomers. The most northerly cluster, at Town Head, includes the Queen's Head Inn, with stone slab floors and a mayoral parlour which has been the scene of Troutbeck's mayor-making ceremony for over 200 years.

Borrowdale

No apologies are made for returning to Borrowdale for the next example of these walks in the dales. The area around Rosthwaite is especially rewarding, both upstream, around Johnny Wood, and lower down the valley, around Castle Crag. Johnny Wood, accessible by a path leading to the cottages at Peathow and to Longthwaite Bridge, is an excellent example of an indigenous Lake District oakwood, and also has a remarkable variety of ferns, liverworts and mosses, plants which thrive here because of the very high rainfall in the area. Downstream from Rosthwaite a path can be followed over New Bridge and close to Pennybridge Dub as far as the quarries in High Hows Wood; close by here is Castle Crag, whose hillfort – certainly in use in Roman times and in the Dark Ages – overlooks an ice marginal channel later utilised for the route of the ancient trackway from Grange into upper Borrowdale. The track approaches Grange through Dalt Wood, but near Gowder Dub a riverside path can be picked up for the return journey to the village of Rosthwaite, on its rocky knoll above the Derwent flood plain.

Langdale

A more ambitious walk takes in the two Langdale valleys, with an impressive array of peaks close at hand, together with visits to two contrasting tarns. Starting at the Old Dungeon Ghyll Hotel, one of the most famous of the climbers' hotels in the district, the walk reaches its first objective, the lonely Blea Tarn, by means of footpaths which climb below Side Pike, with magnificent views into Oxendale and Mickleden, the twin valleys at the head of Great Langdale. A further path leads down to the road from Wrynose Pass as it descends into Little Langdale close to the farm at Fell Foot, sheltering below the 'thing-mount' which is reputed to have been the annual meeting place of the Viking settlers in the two valleys. Immediately ahead is Little Langdale Tarn, in its wide and somewhat unexciting bowl.

Much more attractive is the area below the tarn, with Slater Bridge the highlight. This footbridge across the River Brathay, with its stone slabs linking islands and spanning pools of clear water, was originally constructed by workers in the slate quarries whose remains disfigure the slopes of Wetherlam to the south, and was later used by Lanty Slee, a nineteenth-century whisky smuggler whose illicit stills were located nearby in the Tilberthwaite Fells. From the hamlet of Little Langdale a lane runs past Dale End and pleasantly through Baysbrown Wood to Chapel Stile and Great Langdale; footpaths now lead alongside the Great Langdale Beck, with magnificent views of the Langdale Pikes, to New Dungeon Ghyll, where the overused path to Stickle Tarn begins. Finally a very good green lane at the base of the fells can be used to get back to the Old Dungeon Ghyll, a late-medieval 'statesman' farm but now a pleasant hotel.

THE PASSES

Some of the finest walking in the National Park can be had by tramping the tracks which connect adjacent valleys. No summits are conquered, but the views of the fells are often magnificent and there is a real sense of satisfaction in having followed ancient routes – dating, perhaps, from the packhorse era or from the days of whisky-smuggling – through such dramatic scenery.

Wasdale Head is a focal point for these old tracks: from the cluster of dwellings around the famous inn three routes connect the most dramatic of the western valleys with its neighbours. The head of Ennerdale is reached through Mosedale and across the Black Sail Pass; the well-known Sty Head Pass links Wasdale with Seathwaite in Borrowdale; and the old corpse road across Burnmoor, along which Wasdale Head's departed had to be carried until the dalehead chapel was licensed for burials in the early nineteenth century, provides a route to Boot in Eskdale.

Black Sail

The first of these routes, across the Black Sail Pass to Ennerdale, is a classic of its kind. It starts well, too, passing the delightful Row Bridge, a low packhorse bridge which once carried the valley road from Wasdale Head towards the coastal plain but which now merely conveys walkers (and sheep) into Mosedale. The Black Sail route rises gradually across the flanks of Kirk Fell, with the view ahead dominated by the intimidating bulk of Pillar, which forms the back wall of Mosedale. The best is yet to come, however, for arrival at the summit of the pass reveals the wild head of Ennerdale, together with the afforested slopes of the lower valley and the majestic summits of the High Stile range and Haystacks across the glaciated trench. Between High Crag and Haystacks is the Scarth Gap Pass, the natural extension to the Black Sail route, leading down to Gatesgarth and blessed with a marvellous panorama across Buttermere to the north-western fells.

The Garburn Pass

Towards the eastern fringe of the Lake District is another excellent walk between rather than to the top of the fells. This is based on the Garburn Road, the old packhorse route from Troutbeck to the delightful hamlet of Kentmere. The route follows a line of weakness in the rocks along a thin band of Coniston Limestone which has resisted erosion less well than the rock formations on either side. From Troutbeck church the old road rises as a stony track etched into the hillside and hemmed in by drystone walls as it makes for the low col between Yoke and Sallows. East of the Garburn Pass the track is less eroded and pleasanter underfoot as it descends slowly to the village of Kentmere; to the right can be seen the fourteenth-century pele tower of Kentmere Hall. The packhorse route, surprisingly important in its day, then passed through Green Quarter and along the walled lane above Stile End to Sadgill in Longsleddale, where it crossed the River Sprint on the present, picturesque packhorse bridge before heading either north across the Gatescarth Pass to Mardale or south towards Kendal.

Walna Scar

Many more examples of these passes, some of them at a relatively high altitude and thus exposed to raw winter weather, and others very well used in their heyday, can be identified from a study of the map. The Walna Scar Road, connecting Coniston with Seathwaite in Dunnerdale, is a classic example: a prehistoric routeway passing close to Little Arrow Moor, with its stone circle and Bronze Age burial mounds, it rises to 580m (1,990ft) as it crosses the Walna Scar Pass, the fifth highest in the Lake District. The way lies past the former Coniston railway station and then up to the open moor below the Old Man, passing the virtually dried-up Boo Tarn and then through rock gateways – the popular route to the towering Dow Crag, dominating the barren upland tarn of Goat's Water, forks right near here – before reaching the summit of the pass and the long descent to Seathwaite.

Sticks Pass

Higher still, at 735m (2,420ft) (only Esk Hause is higher) is Sticks Pass, used by packhorses carrying lead ore from Greenside Mine near Glen-ridding to be smelted at Stonycroft, in the Newlands valley, and Brigham near Keswick. The name derives from the tall stakes, long since vanished, which were driven into the ground to mark the line of the track during the worst of the winter weather. At this height the winter snows can be both heavy and prolonged, and indeed the slopes to the south are alive with skiers nowadays when conditions are right. Generally, however, the surroundings at the summit of the pass are bleak and a little dreary, and it is only its elevation and its position in

The route to one of Lakeland's forgotten high-level passes: Sweden Bridge Lane, above Ambleside, leads to the Scandale Pass and eventually to Patterdale

the heart of the Helvellyn range which assures Sticks Pass of real distinction.

Greenup Edge

The well-used path from Borrowdale through the Stonethwaite valley and across Greenup Edge into Easedale and finally to Grasmere passes through an almost equally featureless landscape as it crosses the central watershed of the Lake District, but in its lower reaches to both east and west of this barrier it is quite delightful. Once again this was a busy packhorse route in its time, but it is just as important now as an easy walkers' route into the heart of Borrowdale. Starting from the west, the route passes through the attractive hamlet of Stonethwaite, with its cluster of whitewashed stone farms and cottages, and after crossing Stonethwaite Bridge runs alongside the beck to Smithymire Island, the site of a bloomery established by the monks of Fountains Abbey to smelt their ore, carted along Langstrath from Ore Gap. The way ahead is dominated now by the glorious ramparts of Eagle Crag, but the path lies to the left here, climbing to Greenup Edge and then down into the head of Far Easedale, a place of formidable crags, boulder-strewn slopes and the tumbling waters of the beck in its rocky trench. Lower down the scenery becomes more gentle and the old trade route crosses the beck on Stythwaite Steps before entering the village of Grasmere along a narrow lane.

Grisedale Hause

North-eastwards from Grasmere one of the busiest packhorse routes crossed the Helvellyn massif by means of Grisedale Hause on its way to Patterdale. The track is very clear as it climbs alongside Tongue Gill, passing yet more iron ore mines, to the Hause at 610m (2,004ft). This is the col separating the Helvellyn and Fairfield groups; to the north, beyond the bleak and exposed Grisedale Tarn in its rocky basin, is the path to Dollywaggon Pike, Nethermost Pike and then Helvellyn itself. The way down into Grisedale is steep and rough at first, past Ruthwaite Lodge, originally built in 1854 as a shooting lodge but now in use as a climbing hut, and along the lower slopes of St Sunday Crag to the isolated farmstead of Elmhow. The ancient route crosses the seventeenth-century packhorse bridge here and approaches Patterdale along a surfaced road.

THE LOWER FELLS

In the great rush to conquer the biggest and apparently the best of the Lake District's mountains, the vast majority of walkers visiting the region overlook the fact that some of the choicest routes lead not to the highest summits – some of which provide dull walking in the extreme – but to the tops of the lower fells. These outstanding routes, often uncrowded but always worthwhile, traverse varied and attractive country and offer better views than those available from the heights. Some of the best are included below, though there are many others, most of which can be discovered from the map or from low-level reconnaissance in the dales.

Mellbreak

An obvious example which will be familiar to those whose knowledge of the area extends beyond the tourist traps as far as the delightful western dales is Mellbreak, 510m (1,676ft) high but with the presence of a much higher mountain because it stands alone above the western shore of Crummock Water. The most arresting profile of the fell, though, is not its forbidding frontal assault on the eye from across the lake, but its end-on, pyramid peak aspect from Kirkstile: from here it simply *has* to be climbed. The best route lies along the lane to Kirkhead, then through bracken to the base of Raven Crag. The crag can easily be climbed, keeping away from the gullies and rock faces which confront Crummock Water, across heathery slopes to the north top of the fell. Sadly this is not the summit of Mellbreak: a level walk of about half a mile now follows before the highest point is underfoot. The great advantage of this easy walk across the summit plateau is that a tremendous panorama of the Buttermere fells develops as the walk progresses.

Dodd

The little satellite fell of Dodd usually goes unconsidered amongst the fells in the Skiddaw group, but it is in fact a very fine viewpoint and an easy walk from the Keswick to Carlisle road. Starting from Mirehouse, the route lies alongside the Skill Beck for much of the way, with good views along Bassenthwaite Lake, as far as the col of Long Doors. A wretchedly difficult route over unstable scree leaves from the col to climb Carl Side and eventually Skiddaw, but the way to the top of Dodd is much easier, through a pine wood and over rocks, swampy ground and then easy rocks again. A memorial tablet marks the summit, from which there are excellent views of the central and north-western fells across Derwentwater. A choice of routes along waymarked forest trails now leads back to Mirehouse.

High Rigg

A personal favourite amongst these climbs in the lower fells is the little walk from the church of St John's in the Vale to the adjacent summit of High Rigg, at only 354m (1,163ft) the highest point of the ridge which divides the valleys of St John's Beck and the Naddle Beck. The church, approached along a gated road, is a low, unsophisticated, squat-towered structure, typical of many in the Lakes. The path to the top of High Rigg starts just to the west of the church and climbs steeply for a short distance, ascending a marvellous green rake at one point, before

(overleaf) *The splendid fell of Mellbreak (left) dominating Loweswater on the north-western fringes of the Lake District*

becoming an easy stroll through quite broken terrain to the summit plateau, which is pleasantly rocky and, if the route is well chosen, can entail a little scramble before the highest point is reached.

The views are quite magnificent, from Grasmoor and the Newlands fells in the west through the dominating Skiddaw and Blencathra massifs in the north to the northern ramparts of the Helvellyn range in the east. These surprisingly rocky outliers of Helvellyn itself are usually dismissed as flat-topped and tedious, but their western slopes are of great interest, not least to rock climbers. This interest centres on the detached bastion on the slopes of Watson's Dodd, known as the Castle Rock of Triermain; a remarkable, craggy tor jutting into the valley, it has attracted its share of legend and romance, having been tentatively identified as the site of the Green Chapel in the medieval poem *Sir Gawayne and the Green Knight* and later used by Sir Walter Scott as the setting for *The Bridal of Triermain*.

Eagle Crag

Travellers along the valley road through Borrowdale, journeying between Rosthwaite and Seatoller, have a fine view of our next objective, the proud buttress of Eagle Crag, which stands guard at the head of the Stonethwaite valley, its slopes running down to Smithymire Island at the confluence of Greenup Gill and Langstrath Beck. Although it is hard at first to see any way of tackling the craggy face of the fell, a satisfying direct ascent is in fact perfectly feasible. The way lies across steep grass, bracken, scree and, worst of all, boulder fields to the top of the subsidiary buttress of Bleak How; from here it is comparatively simple to reach the summit of Eagle Crag, though the last steps require some minor scrambling ability. From the cairn many of the major fells can be seen, including Great Gable, Scafell Pike, and Bowfell.

Helm Crag

It is not without a little trepidation that the next example of a fell which makes up for its lack of elevation with sheer style and character is included. This is Helm Crag, one of the most familiar and popular fells in the district. This popularity stems not from the attributes of the walk to its summit, however – though the fact that the National Trust have had to reconstruct the path from Grasmere in its entirety is eloquent testimony to the weight of visitors it suffers – but from the unusual configuration of the summit rocks when seen from the valley below.

Depending on the viewpoint, various scenes can (given sufficient imagination!) be recognised, though the best-known is the Lion and the Lamb. The fell has more to offer, though, for it is set in attractive scenery and it has a delightful summit area, with the top itself accessible only by scrambling up a little rocky peak. Don't expect to have the fell to yourself during the summer months, however.

Hallin Fell

Amongst the fells which crowd in at the head of Ullswater Place Fell holds pride of place as the perfect destination for a short walk, combining relative ease of ascent with interest and variety in the walk itself and with a fine reward at the summit of a marvellous vista of the surrounding scenery, notably Helvellyn above the craggy back wall of the deep hollow containing Red Tarn between the twin aretes of Striding Edge and Swirral Edge. At 656m (2,154ft) it is, sadly, a little too high to qualify as one of the lower fells. Fortunately a fine substitute lies close at hand, in the shape of Hallin Fell.

Hallin Fell's summit is a mere 387m (1,271ft) above sea level, and it can be reached very easily indeed from the newer of Martindale's two churches, yet its situation is delightful, perched above Kailpot Crag and overlooking two reaches of Ullswater. It is slightly detached from the main mountain mass at the head of the lake, and as a result has better views than might be expected. These views are not just related to Ullswater, however: nowhere else has a better situation in relation to Martindale and its tributary valleys, notably the almost deserted glacial trough of Boredale – named after the wild boar, which died out here in the thirteenth century as its woodland habitat was progressively turned over to sheep pastures. From Martindale church a wide grassy path, made slippery in dry weather by the passage of countless boots and shoes, leads straight up to the summit, where there is a magnificent and very substantial cairn, out of all proportion to the importance of the fell itself.

Loughrigg

No description of the best of the lower fells would be complete without reference to Loughrigg Fell, that amorphous mass covering a huge area west of Ambleside and between the Brathay valley and Grasmere. Despite the vast area it covers, Loughrigg's highest point (summit would be too pretentious a description) lies at only about 335m (1,100ft), yet this is a fell to spend time on, with excellent walks on grassy and heathery paths, little crags to explore, and splendid views across the Grasmere bowl, along the length of Windermere and westwards to the Langdale Pikes. The most popular walk traverses Loughrigg Terrace, an excellent promenade above the peaceful lake of Grasmere, but there are others which are equally as interesting, none more so than the north-south traverse from Ellers to Steps End near Rydal. The caves of Loughrigg Quarries, the biggest a massive cavern, are close to the northern end of this attractive walk.

9
HIGH LEVEL WALKS

The high tops of the Lake District have always excited the imagination of walkers – though perhaps too much emphasis has been placed on the very highest. Although Helvellyn is probably the most visited, the other Threethousanders (Scafell Pike, the highest land in England; its near neighbour Scafell; and Skiddaw) are not far behind, and a select few of the other fells are almost as popular. In this group can be included Great Gable, symbol of the National Park, the magnificent Blencathra, and the Langdale Pikes. Yet there are other Lakeland mountains which, though they are more modest in stature, have compensating attractions for the more discerning walker : impressive mountain scenery, superlative views (often far better than those from the highest levels) and, perhaps best of all, the opportunity for quiet enjoyment when the honeypot peaks are thronged with visitors. In this chapter it is only possible to introduce a selection of the best walks in high fell country, some very well known and others of such quality that they deserve to become so.

Mardale and the High Street Range

In the eastern Lake District there are two places in particular to head for, namely Mardale Head and Patterdale. Mardale is of course a drowned valley, its focal point of Mardale Green lost beneath the waters of Haweswater since the 1930s, but the dalehead is the starting point for the best walks in the High Street range.

From Mardale Head probably the most popular walk is the ascent of High Street via the craggy and at times narrow ridge of Long Stile, but there are other routes worthy of consideration. The best, perhaps, takes in Harter Fell, Mardale Ill Bell and Kidsty Pike in addition to High Street, and descends into the ghostly valley of Riggindale. From Mardale Head, where there is limited parking, the way initially lies along the former packhorse trail making for the Gatescarth Pass; at the pass, a rather boggy area overlooking the seldom visited valley of Mosedale, a well-worn path strikes up the slopes of Harter Fell, climbing comfortably to reach the rocky summit plateau, its highest point marked by a cairn now adorned with the twisted remains of the iron fence which once traversed the area. From here there is an awesome panorama into the heart of Lakeland, across the High Street plateau to Helvellyn, the central fells and, in the blue distance, the Scafell range.

Mardale Ill Bell is the next objective, easily reached via the Nan Bield Pass, where another packhorse route comes up steeply on its way from Kentmere past the delightful tarn of Small Water, where there are some unusual low shelters, to Mardale Head. Keep to the right on the way up the slopes of Mardale Ill Bell to enjoy the best of the views, both down the valley past Small Water and Haweswater to the Pennines and also across the bleak upland tarn of Blea Water, the deepest tarn in the district, into the heart of the High Street range. Once the summit of Mardale Ill Bell has been reached the way forward becomes much less rocky, and a vast sheepwalk has to be traversed on the way to High Street, at 828m (2,718ft) the highest point in the ridge which bears its name. So flat and grassy is the area that it also bears the name of Racecourse Hill, and the annual Mardale shepherds' meet and fair day was held up here until 1835.

Northwards from High Street's summit the ridge narrows dramatically at the Straits of Riggindale, where the walkers' path and former Roman road converge. To the left is the deep Hayeswater valley, to the right the deep bowl of Riggindale, a classic example of a U-shaped glaciated valley, while straight ahead the High Street ridge, going on towards High Raise, throws off a subsidiary spur to The Knott and Rest Dodd. Our route lies to the right, leaving the main High Street ridge and climbing gently to the summit of Kidsty Pike, perched above the steep and rocky northern side of Riggindale. The eastern spur of Kidsty Pike is then descended to the shores of Haweswater, and the final stage of the walk consists of a gentle stroll around the head of the lake, passing

Ill Bell and Kentmere Reservoir from the slopes of Harter Fell. The old packhorse track from Kentmere across the Nan Bield Pass to Mardale ascends the slopes on the extreme right

the site of the former Riggindale Farm and rounding The Rigg, the wooded spur at the foot of Long Stile, on the way to Mardale Head.

Patterdale and Helvellyn

Patterdale is much better known than Mardale, and is wonderfully situated at the head of Ullswater, surrounded by fine mountains, from Place Fell and St Sunday Crag round to Helvellyn. The classic Helvellyn route, up Striding Edge and down Swirral Edge, begins here.

After an easy tramp across the Grisedale fellside the walker encounters Striding Edge, best known though perhaps not quite the best of Lakeland's aretes. This very narrow ridge between Nethermost Cove and Red Tarn Cove – the latter with Red Tarn itself, the only tarn stocked with the rare schelly and backed by a tremendous cliff reaching right up to the summit plateau of Helvellyn itself – is a popular though easily under-estimated route, with plenty of opportunity for rock scrambling and a real feeling of achievement when the main

Helvellyn ridge is reached. Now there is a straightforward walk to the summit of Helvellyn, at 950m (3,118ft) the second highest in the Lake District, with its clutter of cairns, shelter, OS pillar and monuments.

The way down Swirral Edge, on bare rock to begin with, is highly attractive and not too difficult, with Red Tarn sparkling in its ice-deepened hollow far below. A path heading for the tarn leaves the ridge but it is preferable to keep to the heights as far as the top of Catstycam, a pyramid peak at the end of the ridge. The northern face of Catstycam falls away in a tumbling mass of shattered rock and scree to the corrie which used to contain Keppelcove Tarn (a former reservoir for the Greenside lead mine, this has been dry since 1927, when it broke its banks in a storm), but the return to Patterdale descends the east shoulder of the fell and joins the Red Tarn path down to the Glenridding Beck and past the buildings of the Greenside mine. The beck here flows through delightful ravines, with rowans clinging tenaciously to rock faces which fall sheer into the clear water. Beyond the mine a level path diverges from the beck to reach Miresbeck, the slopes of Keldas (a good viewpoint for Ullswater), the secret Lanty's Tarn, and the lane alongside Grisedale Beck into Patterdale.

The Fairfield Horseshoe

A very good introduction to the eastern fells, this is a popular and not too difficult walk which is also highly accessible, starting in the old part of Ambleside with a lovely walk to High Sweden Bridge. As the walled lane rises above the town the views open out, taking in the length of Windermere to the south and the Rydal valley, backed by the Langdale Pikes, to the west. Closer at hand the lane passes through little woods and runs alongside the Scandale Beck before crossing it on the highly photogenic single-arched High Sweden Bridge. A stiff pull up the fellside now leads to the summits of Low Pike and, not too far distant, its bigger brother High Pike. The way to the next objective, Dove Crag, lies close to the head of the tremendous side valley of Dovedale, a wild trench ringed with magnificent crags. This is real mountain country, rocky and desolate, and the route now takes in a high-level traverse of Hart Crag on the way past the head of Deepdale to the summit of Fairfield.

The great glory of Fairfield is its northern face, with projecting buttresses falling dramatically into Deepdale, so it is worth diverting along the subsidiary ridge to Cofa Pike in order to obtain the best views. Down below, to the west, lies Grisedale Tarn, a well-known staging

High Sweden Bridge, a classic packhorse bridge across Scandale Beck on the path from Ambleside to Low Pike and the Fairfield Horseshoe

post on the old packhorse route from Grasmere to Patterdale, while to the north are the flanks of Dollywaggon Pike, the first of the outliers of Helvellyn. There are excellent views not only of the tremendous Helvellyn massif but also of Place Fell and the far eastern fells around High Street. The Fairfield Horseshoe turns south, however, along the top of Fairfield Brow to Greatrigg Man and then easily down the ridge on a carpet of grass to Heron Pike, Nab Scar (which still has the remains of a medieval deer park boundary) and Rydal, before returning at valley level through Rydal Park to Ambleside.

Blencathra and Skiddaw

It is not by mistake that Blencathra is listed before Skiddaw, despite its lesser height; in terms of interest and quality of walking there is no real comparison between the two. Skiddaw has generally smooth slopes and relatively few points of high drama – though the sight of the central fells from Skiddaw Little Man is memorable, and the cascading Whitewater

Dash to the left of Dead Crags is a gem known to too few. Blencathra has not only its dramatically serrated southern face, with a succession of ridges – the best of them Hall's Fell, narrowing to the arete of Narrow Edge in its upper reaches – and intervening ravines, but also the even narrower knife-edged ridge of Sharp Edge, perched alluringly above the supposedly bottomless Scales Tarn.

The best way to the base of Hall's Fell cuts diagonally through fields from Threlkeld, passing a substantial field barn on the way to Gategill, site of a former mining venture and now the place where the Blencathra foxhounds are kennelled. A path climbs beside Gate Gill to the fell gate and a view of some of the derelict mine buildings. Now the climb up Hall's Fell begins, steeply at first on exposed slaty rock but later more steadily through heather to reach Narrow Edge. A narrow path runs along the right hand side of the arete, a little below the crest, but even this is rocky and a little exposed, with dramatic views down into the depths of Doddick Gill. The more adventurous will elect for the sensational scrambling route along the crest itself, with Gate Gill steeply down to the left and the summit of Blencathra itself in sight at the top of the arete. Once the slabs, miniature rock towers and little crags have been conquered the summit, beautifully poised at the edge of the abyss, is gained by a final scramble up loose rock. John Ruskin may have come this way: he included 'several bits of real crag work' in his ascent of the mountain.

Probably the finest conclusion to such a walk is a descent along Sharp Edge, with Scales Tarn poised below, but many might feel that Narrow Edge is exertion enough and will opt to descend Blue Screes to reach the col at the head of the Glenderamackin valley. Turn right here and accompany the infant stream, here at the start of its extraordinary journey to Mungrisdale and then sharply round Souther Fell to the far side of Blencathra. There is a very good, well graded and pleasantly surfaced path all the way down to Mungrisdale, though in order to get back to Threlkeld it is necessary to leave this and climb up to the col at the head of Mousthwaite Comb before curving round to Scales and, by paths at the base of the south face, Threlkeld.

Skiddaw by the 'tourist' path from Keswick, across Jenkin Hill and Skiddaw Little Man, is a straightforward route which can be kept under foot most of the year simply by following the party in front, but it lacks real interest during the route because of the nature of Skiddaw – steep in places but without rock outcrops or the like to enliven the scene. The alert explorer can, however, find a number of alternatives of rather greater subtlety. From the north, a worthwhile route takes the Skiddaw

The dramatic higher slopes of Narrow Edge on the Hall's Fell route to the top of Blencathra – the shadowed peak on the horizon

House road as far as the foot of Dead Crags, then skirts them to gain the summit of Bakestall and continue up the north ridge to the top of Skiddaw itself. Another possibility is to start at the Ravenstone Hotel and climb The Edge to Ullock Pike before traversing Longside Edge, a quite sharp arete, to Carl Side; but scree-ridden slopes now have to be ascended on the way to Skiddaw Little Man and Skiddaw. Other quite pleasant routes start at Millbeck and Applethwaite, and a final possibility is to opt out of the mainstream altogether and head up the eastern slopes from the former shepherd's cottage at Skiddaw House, in its dramatically isolated position in the grassy wastes of Skiddaw Forest.

Newlands

The Newlands Round, though it is likely to be reasonably well populated in the season, seems not to have captured the imagination of walkers in the same way as, say, the Fairfield or Mosedale Horseshoes and as a result can be enjoyed quietly and at leisure. Start at Little Town and take the excellent green path into Yewthwaite Combe, with fine retrospective views to Causey Pike and its neighbours. On reaching the ridge at Hause Gate, turn right to climb steadily up towards the summit of Maiden Moor. Progress is likely to be slow, not because of undue difficulties underfoot but because the panorama eastwards and northwards is spectacular. Derwentwater lies spread out below, with Catbells in front and to the left of the spreading bulk of Skiddaw, and Blencathra's magnificent southern face well seen across the lake. To the east the knobbly fells above Grange-in-Borrowdale form a foreground for the Helvellyn range.

On the way to High Spy a particular highlight as the path skirts above Eel Crags is the sight of the deep, shady gullies on the far side of the Newlands valley. Then the path, easily followed and quite stony in places, dips down to Dalehead Tarn before climbing very steeply up to the outstandingly attractive cairn at the summit of Dale Head, almost overhanging the crags at the head of Newlands. The panorama is superb, from Helvellyn round to the Central Fells, the High Stile ridge and, best of all, straight down the trough of Newlands to Swinside and Bassenthwaite Lake. The ridge west from Dale Head is one of the highlights of the walk, with the deep Buttermere valley away to the left and the summits of Hindscarth and Robinson easily gained. Robinson, its name derived rather prosaically from a former landowner, has the oddest of summits, with two narrow and parallel ribs of rock snaking across the otherwise grassy top of the fell.

A further surprise awaits on the descent along the north ridge of Robinson, for in descending Blea Crags the route lies down a succession of steep rock staircases close to a quite precipitous drop into Keskadale. The way now lies down High Snab Bank and into the Scope Beck valley, following a lane to Newlands church, beautifully situated on open ground with a backdrop of fells, and with the former schoolhouse adjoining. The starting point for the walk is now only a short stroll away, across the Newlands Beck and along a narrow lane to the tiny cluster of cottages and farms at Little Town.

The Langdale Pikes

Few visitors to the National Park will be unaware of the Langdale Pikes, old favourites to many and instantly recognisable as a cluster of prominent rocky summits above the U-shaped valley of Great Langdale. The ascent from the New Dungeon Ghyll Hotel, though not one for the seeker after solitude, nevertheless remains the classic route; the considerable and commendable repair work on the footpaths ascending by Mill Gill (often glamorised as Stickle Ghyll) is testimony to the pounding the paths here take. There is a choice of paths, on either side of the stream, though they converge at the outlet of Stickle Tarn, a corrie lake much enlarged when it was harnessed as a reservoir for the Elterwater gunpowder works but still natural-looking and with a fearsome back wall comprising the magnificent crags of Pavey Ark. Skirt the tarn to the right, then ascend Pavey Ark by one of three routes.

By far the most remarkable is Jack's Rake, which can easily be picked out ascending diagonally and steeply from right to left; it is the hardest route in the Lake District in common use by mere walkers, since it does not have much in the way of protection in places, and only the more acrobatic should attempt it. An easier but still interesting alternative uses the gully climbing slightly left to right from close to the start of Jack's Rake, and reaching the summit by means of a rough, steep but far less exposed climb. Finally, the less sure-footed or ambitious can take a path climbing up by Bright Beck and then cut up behind the crags, still on quite steep rocks in places, to reach the top of Pavey Ark.

Most of the hard climbing has now been completed, though on the traverse to Harrison Stickle, the highest of the Langdale Pikes at 732m (2,403ft), it is possible to devise another scrambling route on easy rocks. The way now lies across hummocky and bouldery ground to Loft Crag – the top of the awesome Gimmer Crag, another early climbers' haunt, is close at hand here – and Pike o' Stickle. It is quite feasible to descend here into the upper reaches of the scree gully where the most famous of all the axe factories was located, and even to find the man-made cave in the south buttress which may have been hacked out by the Neolithic axe-makers, but the ground is steep and dangerously loose and it is preferable to keep to the plateau across the edge of Martcrag Moor, close to its Langdale edge, as far as the path coming up over the Stake Pass from Langstrath. Well-defined zigzags then lead down into Mickleden, one of the two branches of upper Great Langdale, and along the very popular path to the Old Dungeon Ghyll Hotel (its real ale very tempting at this stage of the walk!) and, below Raven Howe, New Dungeon Ghyll.

The Coniston Fells

Shunned by many because they appear to lack the excitement of the Central Fells, the Coniston Fells deserve far better because they combine dramatic rock faces with stretches of easy high-level walking and also possess a strong sense of history, from the evidence of prehistoric man on Little Arrow Moor to the remains of Coniston's industrial past in Coppermines Valley. Best seen from Torver High Common, where Dow Crag and the Old Man of Coniston rise steeply from the moorland plateau, or from across Coniston Water, this compact group of fells is full of surprises for the explorer and the Coniston round described here is a richly rewarding walk for the energetic.

Leave Coniston along the Walna Scar Road, a prehistoric trackway at the base of the fells, and pass the virtually extinct Boo Tarn and a little spring called Well in Crag. The way lies through two rock gateways, then divides: the easier route, to the left, follows the track to the Walna Scar Pass (at 605m (1,990ft) the fifth highest in the National Park) before turning up the fellside to Brown Pike and Dow Crag, whilst the right-hand alternative reaches Goat's Water in its desolate, rocky basin at the foot of the scree fans and astonishing rock buttresses making up the tremendous eastern face of Dow Crag. Rock scramblers will enjoy making their way to the summit via the easiest of the gullies, the so-called South Rake, but others will make for Goat's Hause on the ridge connecting Dow Crag to the Old Man of Coniston. The top of the Old Man, easily conquered from here, is unlikely to be deserted, though it is dramatically sited, with the corrie tarn of Low Water far below and a magnificent southerly prospect over the estuaries of the Kent, Leven and Duddon.

Now the easy high-level walking along the spine of the Coniston Fells begins, over the rounded dome of Brim Fell to the col at Levers Hause (a quick return to Coniston leaves to the right here, passing Levers Water and the copper mines) and the summits of Swirl How and Great Carrs. While on this broad and level upland sheepwalk it is worth taking the trouble to visit the top of Grey Friar, not for its pretensions as a destination in itself but for the fabulous view of the entire Scafell range across the head of Eskdale, from Slight Side through Scafell, the deep cleft of Mickledore and Scafell Pike to Great End. This means a retracing of steps, back to the top of Swirl How, but this is quickly and painlessly achieved and the final summit, Wetherlam, can now be claimed. The walk curves around the ridge of Prison Band, with the shattered rim of Broad Slack, a massive corrie containing the remains of an aeroplane which failed to clear the ridge, down on the right.

Wetherlam is perhaps the most interesting of all the Coniston Fells. Its industrial past is all too evident in places, with the waste heaps of mineral working on its Tilberthwaite and Little Langdale slopes, and the whole fell pockmarked with adits and mine shafts; Moss Rigg Quarry, the largest of all the holes, is still in production. The summit ridge is met by three parallel north-south ridges (Black Sails, Lad Stones and Yewdale), and the return to Coniston takes the middle one of these, a marvellous open walk with good views to the south over Coniston Water. At the base of the ridge the Coppermines Valley track comes in from the right and this is used as far as Miner's Bridge, where Church Beck is crossed and followed down through wooded, rocky glades to Coniston.

Great Gable and Pillar

These are two favourite mountains, and rightly so, for each has special characteristics which remain long in the memory. Great Gable (simply 'Gable' to many) has the rock architecture of the Great Napes, including Napes Needle, and Gable Crag, while Pillar has Pillar Rock, an awe-inspring buttress falling vertically into the depths of Ennerdale. Both are tackled most frequently, and with good reason, from Wasdale Head, though Great Gable is also a target for many in Borrowdale or at Honister, and Pillar is the climax of an exhilarating though quite long walk over Haycock from Ennerdale.

Wasdale Head, a tiny hamlet but one with a unique place in climbing history, is virtually surrounded by high mountains, but Great Gable cries out to be climbed. Perfectly seen from the hamlet, it promises a magnificent climb and indeed delivers several, with a wide choice of routes. The best require a little perseverance to begin with, as the scree slopes of Gavel Neese are overcome, but the rock pinnacle known as Moses' Finger signals the start of the excitement. It is possible to keep straight ahead, scrambling over the rocky upper sections of Gavel Neese, but this is a tortuous and at times difficult route. Better is the traverse to the right, towards the Great Napes and then energetically up one of the two prominent scree funnels, graphically described as the Great and Little Hell Gates. Better still, in the view of a good number, is the left-hand route, on a level path above the Gable Beck. This is Moses' Trod, reputedly first devised as a whisky smugglers' route from Honister to the coast but certainly much in use in the early days of quarrying at Honister, when the slate was hauled on sledges along this track into Wasdale.

Moses' Trod eventually arrives at Beck Head, the col between Kirk Fell and Great Gable, where there will be either one or two tarns depending on the season. A really enjoyable route involving a little scrambling now rises by the side of Gable Crag to the rocky summit plateau of Great Gable, a place of pilgrimage for many and the highly appropriate site of the Fell and Rock Climbing Club's war memorial. The views along Wasdale from the Westmorland Cairn should be savoured before the return to Wasdale Head, perhaps via the Breast Route to Sty Head and then along the quieter of the paths along the Lingmell Beck valley, is finally tackled.

The way to Pillar lies along the track starting behind the Wasdale Head Inn, passing (but not crossing) an excellent example of a Lakeland packhorse bridge and then striking up alongside the Mosedale Beck towards the Black Sail Pass. At the pass, where there are still the forlorn remains of a gateway, the path to Looking Stead and Pillar climbs up to the left. Looking Stead is as good a vantage point as any for the Forestry Commission's plantations in Ennerdale; clear felling of the drab green blanket, so unfeelingly and unimaginatively imposed on the valley in the 1920s, at least gives them a second chance to get it right. Beyond Looking Stead the High Level Route to Pillar contours across the fellside to Robinson's Cairn, the ideal viewpoint for the east face of Pillar Rock, a savage piece of rock scenery dropping vertically for some 150m (500ft) into Pillar Cove. John Atkinson, a local shepherd, is credited with the first ascent of Pillar Rock, in 1862, and there are now some awesomely difficult routes to the top of the remarkable buttresses and deeply riven gullies which comprise the face of the precipice.

From Robinson's Cairn the Shamrock Traverse, an exciting though not particularly exacting walk for the sure-footed, leads above tremendous crags to a steep scree slope – with fine views of the little rocky tower of Pisgah – and then up to the summit plateau of Pillar. This is a bit of an anti-climax, with the top of the fell a surprisingly level area adorned with cairns, wind-shelters and an Ordnance Survey pillar as well as a ruinous fence, part of a boundary fence which once enclosed the whole of the Ennerdale watershed. The walk continues along the ridge to Scoat Fell, dropping down first to Wind Gap, with the superb sight of Steeple, its summit attainable from the ridge only by scrambling along a rocky arete, across Mirk Cove. A variety of routes confronts the walker bound for Wasdale Head from Scoat Fell; the easiest drops down to Scoat Tarn and the Nether Beck valley, but it is better to gird up the loins for one final ascent and return via Red Pike, its rocky top overlooking the deep glaciated trough of Mosedale, and the col at Dore Head, where a rough scree slope can be used to reach valley level.

Scafell and Scafell Pike

Wasdale Head is also the natural starting point for walkers intent on reaching England's highest point, the summit of Scafell Pike, but there are several other approaches worthy of consideration. Borrowdale and Great Langdale spring immediately to mind, but the best way of all is perhaps the route from Brotherilkeld in upper Eskdale. This is a long but outstandingly satisfying expedition which passes through a wide variety of mountain scenery, from the relative calm of the Esk valley and the strange bowl of Great Moss to the bouldery chaos of the Scafell Pike plateau.

Brotherilkeld, the highest point of settlement in the dale, was the centre of operations in Eskdale for the Furness monks from 1242 onwards and is nowadays a long, low and above all isolated farmhouse dating mostly from the seventeenth century; it is also the location for the Eskdale Show, usually held on the last Saturday in September. The walk up alongside the Esk from the farm is a delight, with the river rippling through rocky pools and little gorges and the dale closed in by scree slopes and rocky bluffs such as Yew Crags, its name a reminder of the trees which were abundant here before the sheep moved in. At Throstle Garth, the path crosses the single-arched Lingcove Bridge close to the monks' sheepfold and keeps above the river (a detour is necessary to see Esk Falls) as far as the huge basin of Great Moss.

Great Moss was the site of a shallow lake scoured out during the Ice Ages and it is now a peat bog, presenting a real challenge to the walker who likes to remain dryshod; the most promising route uses the medieval boundary wall, a turf bank with a core of boulders, which the monks built in 1284 to restrict their sheep to the lowland pastures whilst allowing the more agile deer to roam freely. Next, the River Esk, shallow and wide hereabouts, has to be crossed, before a route rising diagonally to the right up the steep fellside opposite is taken to reach the delightful and little known summit of Pen. It is then a relatively easy matter to contour round into the upper reaches of Little Narrowcove and thus gain the summit plateau of Scafell Pike across a sea of awkward boulders. This, at 977m (3,206ft), is the highest land in England, though the immediate surroundings are bleak and inhospitable, and not enhanced by the tumbledown wallshelter around the summit. But the walk down to Mickledore and subsequent conquest of Scafell more than makes up for any disappointment.

The approach to Mickledore, a deep col where less resistant volcanic rocks have been rapidly eaten away, reveals the majestic Scafell Crag, a

Scafell Pike and (in mist) Scafell from across Wastwater. The profile of Scafell Crag is especially prominent

splendid piece of rock architecture which bars direct access to Scafell's summit but has one weakness, the rocky gully of Lord's Rake between the main crag and Shamrock Buttress. This has long been a favourite route for adventurous walkers and is showing signs of wear and tear, with a river of scree filling the dead-straight channel which rises steeply from the foot of Deep Gill. Shortly before the first col the West Wall Traverse branches off and forms a suitably exciting climax to the ascent

of a fine mountain. An easier alternative is to keep to the Rake as it rises and falls across the face of the mountain (don't be tempted to detour left into an apparently promising gully; this ends in a desperate scramble) before reaching the summit plateau a little below the highest point, marked by a substantial cairn. The return to Eskdale can then be achieved via Foxes Tarn (the second highest in the district) and the Mickledore path back down to Great Moss and Brotherilkeld or, for those able to finish the walk lower down Eskdale, over Slight Side to Wha House or Boot. Whichever finishing point is chosen, this is a memorable long walk, undoubtedly amongst the best in the Lake District's highest fells.

GAZETTEER

Ambleside has perhaps succumbed too much to tourism, but given the town's superb location this was inevitable and the wonder is that there is still so much to see. Best of all, perhaps, is the oldest part of the town, in narrow streets climbing above the flood plain of the River Rothay to Above Stock; the former chapel of St Anne's, the old house of How Head, the grey slate farmhouses and the Golden Rule, a marvellously unspoilt pub, make a fine combination. Less attractive are the overcrowded market place, with its myriad gift shops, and the Bridge House, possibly built in the seventeenth century as a summerhouse for Ambleside Hall but now just one of the National Trust's odder properties. The parish church, built in the 1850s and designed by Sir Giles Gilbert Scott, is the successor to the chapel in Above Stock. A number of mills can be seen: the Old Mill, now a pottery, was formerly a corn mill and dates from the fourteenth century, while a converted bobbin mill can be seen upstream, together with the remains of mill races. Still further upstream is Stockghyll Force, much visited by the early tourists and in a pleasantly wooded ravine but for all that a minor waterfall. At Waterhead there is a steamer service along the length of Windermere, while at the head of the lake are the remains of Ambleside's precursor, the Roman fort of Galava. Amongst the many events in the town's calendar are the Ambleside Sports, held on the Thursday before the first Monday in July, and the rushbearing ceremony, which takes place on the first Saturday in July.

Askham, attractively situated above the Lowther valley, is a particularly good example of an Anglian green village, with farms and cottages set around a long, narrow central green. The village was one of several purchased by the Lowthers when they were ensconced in the nearby castle and at the height of their power in the eighteenth century. Little survives from before this period, though Askham Hall dates in part from the fourteenth century.

Backbarrow is an industrial hamlet in the Leven valley, with the remains of the most ambitious of Lakeland's iron furnaces, originally built in 1711, and other relics of the heyday of water power. The 'Dolly Blue' works closed only recently and has been converted into an hotel and timeshare complex.

Bampton is an unremarkable village in the Lowther valley, passed through by many on their way to Haweswater reservoir and Mardale Head. The name of the pub, the St Patrick's Well Inn, recalls the legend that St Patrick walked to Bampton after having been shipwrecked on Duddon Sands in 540AD. The nearby hamlet of Bampton Grange was originally an outlying farm of Shap Abbey.

Bassenthwaite village not only stands well away from the lake of the same name, but it is also shunned by the two churches with which its name is associated. The older of the two, that of St Bega, lies two miles to the south, along an unmade track by the lake shore; it has a Norman chancel arch but little else escaped the Victorian restorers. St John, an elaborate edifice of 1878, is situated close to the village school in the hamlet of Chapel. The centre of the village, though, is the irregular green around which a mixture of slate-grey cottages and newer houses cluster.

Bassenthwaite Lake, though it sits prettily at the foot of Skiddaw's western outliers and is especially attractive when seen from them (the view down the lake from the little subsidiary peak of Dodd is reasonably accessible and very pleasant), is really too far divorced from the central core of the Lake District to yield a great deal which is spectacular. Some four miles in length and fourth largest of the lakes, it has the fast, noisy A66 along the bulk of its western shore and is perhaps best approached from the east, either at Bassenthwaite's older church or near Mirehouse, where the house and grounds are open at certain times. The northern section of the lake is used by the Bassenthwaite Sailing Club. Since 1979 the lake has been owned by the Lake District Special Planning Board.

Black Combe is the forgotten fell of the Lake District, its smooth slopes covering a huge area in the extreme south-west yet so far removed from the mountain core as to be scarcely glimpsed from most of the central fells. Yet it is of unusual interest, being composed of an outcrop of Skiddaw Slates encircled by Borrowdale Volcanics, and with one of the Lake District's rare stone circles on the slopes of its north-eastern spur, Swinside Fell. Monk Foss, at the foot of its western slopes, was one of Furness Abbey's properties until 1242, when it passed into the hands of David de Mulcaster. Wordsworth was sufficiently impressed to write a poem about the fell in 1813 – *View from the top of Black Combe*.

Blea Tarn must be the most common tarn name in the district – though arguably the best is actually called Blea Water; this one is the deepest of all the tarns and nestles in a corrie plucked out of the higher slopes of High Street and Mardale Ill Bell. The best known Blea Tarn sits in an upland hollow between Great Langdale and Little Langdale, is owned by the National Trust, and has excellent and striking views of the Langdale Pikes.

Blencathra, still occasionally called Saddleback after the distinctive profile of the summit plateau, is one of the great mountains of Britain, with a succession of splendid routes up the ridges and intervening gullies which make up its distinctive southern face and, tucked around its eastern flank, the spectacular rocky arete of Sharp Edge above Scales Tarn. The best of the southern approaches is from Gategill, ascending Hall's Fell and the exciting Narrow Edge to arrive exactly at the summit. Blencathra's name is of Celtic origin, and so too is that of the Glenderamackin, the river which meanders around its northern, eastern and southern flanks; the walk along the valley on a green path from Mungrisdale is delightful. To the west the Glenderaterra Beck divides Blencathra from Skiddaw.

Boot is a splendid base for exploring upper Eskdale, with two inns (the Burnmoor and, somewhat away from the hamlet, the Woolpack, formerly catering for the packhorse trains) and a variety of other accommodation. There is plenty to be seen in and around the hamlet: the remains of iron ore mines, the packhorse bridge over the Whillan Beck and the adjacent corn mill, painstakingly restored and now open to the public, and the chapel of St Catherine, down by the River Esk, here at its most delightful with wooded banks, rocky gorges and stepping stones. A fine walk leaves Boot over the packhorse bridge, then climbs alongside the beck to reach Burnmoor, with its burial mounds, secluded tarn and excellent views towards and across Wasdale.

Borrowdale is the Lake District dale *par excellence*, with a classic lake, with its gentle sylvan beauty, giving way to the rugged slopes of dramatic fells higher up the dale. There is something for everyone, notably the sight of Derwentwater from a whole series of splendid if somewhat hackneyed viewpoints such as Friar's Crag, Ashness Bridge or the Surprise View, the subdued and intricate landscape of the mid-valley around Rosthwaite and Stonethwaite, and the fellwalkers' paradise around Seathwaite, with paths striking off in all directions at the start of classic expeditions to Great Gable, Great End, Scafell Pike and the other major peaks. But there is much more – the unusual, such as the glacial erratic known as the Bowder Stone; the picturesque, including the Lodore Falls; and the historic, represented by the hillfort on Castle Crag. Rock climbers will make for Shepherd's Crag, botanists for Johnny Wood, with its ferns and liverworts, and others for man-made attractions such as the bridge at Grange-in-Borrowdale.

Bowfell, though it is seen to advantage from Langstrath, where its bleak northern cliffs stand above Angle Tarn, and from upper Eskdale, where the mountain takes on the appearance of a rocky pyramid, really belongs to Langdale, and is probably climbed most frequently from there, along the rising slopes of The Band to Three Tarns – a desolate and windswept spot between Bowfell and Crinkle Crags – and then either direct to the summit or, more excitingly, along the climbers' traverse below Flat Crag and the jagged outline of Cambridge Crag to the awesome Bowfell Buttress. The top of Bowfell is a jumbled mass of naked rock, with a nice little rocky pyramid for the summit itself. The views are exceptional, too, with a very good profile of the Scafell range and a long prospect down the Esk valley to the Irish Sea.

Bowness, which has now coalesced with Windermere town, is the closer of the two to the lake and has therefore developed a considerable range of facilities for the tourists who congregate here. It does still have its attractions, however, with a pleasant town centre behind the promenade at Bowness Bay, where there is a steamer pier and a variety of boats for hire. Here too is a theatre and a steamboat museum. Nearby Adelaide Hill has a very good overall view of Windermere lake.

Braithwaite has seen a good deal of recent housing development and has not grown in attractiveness as a result. This was the original location of the Cumberland Pencil Company, which began here in 1868 but moved to Keswick thirty years later after a disastrous fire. The Coledale Inn was at one time the factory manager's house. Now the village has a rather suburban feel to it – Keswick is close at hand along the intrusive A66, which bypasses Braithwaite – though it is nicely situated at the foot of the Whinlatter Pass and the ascent of Grisedale Pike, a very worthwhile expedition, starts not far from the village.

Brotherilkeld is the highest farm in Eskdale (though Taw House across the Esk is not too far downstream) and has been so since it was first established by the Norse settlers. The farm was sold to the monks of Furness Abbey in 1242 and has since functioned as the centre of a massive sheep-rearing enterprise. The present farmhouse, long, low and white, dates from the great rebuilding in the Lake District during the heyday of the statesmen farmers in the seventeenth century. A magnificent walk hereabouts follows the Esk upstream to Lingcove Bridge; at higher level the Hardknott Roman fort can also be reached without too much difficulty.

Brothers Water, shallow, reed-fringed and small, is sometimes regarded as a reservoir because of its straight shorelines but is in fact a natural lake at the head of the Patterdale valley, close to the picturesque village of Hartsop and at the foot of the climb to the Kirkstone Pass. The lake was once a great deal larger, and its straight southern shore represents the edge of a mass of deposited material which fills the valley as far as the mouth of Dovedale. It is possible, too, that Brothers Water was once joined to Ullswater; certainly there is a narrow, flat valley floor between the two lakes. Few walkers visit the lake, though there is access to the western side, and the added interest of prehistoric homesteads close at hand.

Broughton-in-Furness is a small market town in lower Dunnerdale, with a spacious market place created in the late eighteenth century, about a hundred years after the market was first established there. There is still a market on Tuesdays, but there is little else to give the feel of a town, and the trade brought by the local woollen and woodland industries has completely disappeared. The curious will seek out the plaque commemorating the laying out of the market square, the obelisk to John Gilpin, who provided the necessary land, the clock which survives from the same period, and Broughton Tower, the seat of the Broughton family from late Saxon days.

Burnmoor, a low plateau separating Wasdale and Eskdale, is a pleasant spot for a short walk from the hamlet of Boot, climbing alongside the Whillan Beck and then along the Old Corpse Road along which the dead were carried from Wasdale Head to St Catherine's chapel at Boot in the days before Wasdale Head's little chapel was licensed for burials. Amongst the items of interest are an old mill site in the Whillan Beck valley, burial mounds to the west of the path, and Burnmoor Tarn, one of the larger tarns in a desolate setting, with Yewbarrow and the fells of the Mosedale Horseshoe peeping over the horizon. By the tarn there is a former hunting lodge, a remote and forbidding building; more cheerful are the ponies which frequent the moor.

Buttermere is the name of a lake, a dale and a small village. The lake is one of awesome beauty, perfectly proportioned in a mountain bowl below the High Stile range, Haystacks, Fleetwith Pike (especially well seen from across the lake, with its spinal ridge rising inexorably at the head of the valley) and Robinson. The circular lakeside walk is easy, restful and full of superb views. From the chapel above the village the harmony of lake and fell can be studied at leisure: above the lake and the wooded lower slopes are considerable corries such as Birkness Comb and Bleaberry Comb, savage crags and, issuing from hanging valleys, cascading streams such as Sour Milk Gill opposite the village. Buttermere village is a little disappointing, though there is a chapel, a post office, a couple of hotels – one of them, the Bridge, formerly known as the Victoria, began life as a corn mill – and a cluster of farm buildings.

Caldbeck is a fascinating large village well off the beaten track on the northern fringes of the National Park, best known for its association with the huntsman John Peel. Above the village there is a deep, narrow limestone gorge (The Howk) in which there was formerly a bobbin mill, destroyed by fire, and closer to the village itself the derelict buildings of Caldbeck woollen mill serve as a further reminder of the industrial past of the area. John Peel, born in 1776, is buried in the churchyard; the song 'D'ye ken John Peel' was written by his friend John Woodcott Graves.

Calder Abbey is pleasantly located in the valley meadows of the River Calder, but it has not always been so peaceful here, and the monks were twice forced to flee by Scottish raiders in the twelfth century. The ruins of the abbey, founded by the order of Savigny in 1134 and later under Cistercian control, are considerable but are not open to the public. The tower stands to half its original 40m (130ft) height, and five bays of the north aisle survive, together with the transept arches and part of the chancel. The monks played a considerable part in the agricultural colonisation of the wild, remote Copeland Forest area, and the remains of their packhorse bridge (Matty Benn's Bridge) higher up the Calder valley offer just one indication of their activity in this area.

Carrock Fell, which contrasts starkly with many of its neighbours in Back o' Skidda' country, is a geological oddity, based on volcanic gabbro and granophyre rather than the Skiddaw Slates which have produced the smoother surrounding fells. The fell stands right at the north-eastern edge of the Lake District and there are substantial views across the Caldew plain and the Eden valley, but the twin treasures of the fell are smaller-scale: a hillfort and a mining venture. The surprisingly extensive remains of the hillfort decorate the summit plateau; the walls still stand to a height of over a metre (3 to 4 feet), though there are gaps in places which represent either gateways or the slighting of the fort by the Romans. The fort, the largest in Cumbria, covers about five acres and appears to have been thrown up in the Iron Age. The mining venture is much more recent, having been started as recently as 1854. It was particularly successful during World War I, when its tungsten ores were in great demand, but subsequent exploitation has been sporadic, although more than twenty minerals have been identified in the vicinity of the mine. A minor road from Mosedale can be taken by those wishing to explore the area.

Cartmel, just outside· the National Park, is a particularly pleasant village (adjudged best-kept village in Cumbria on several occasions) with a good deal of interest. The village square and old water pump, the courtyards of artisans' houses and especially the Norman priory church are among the highlights. National Hunt race meetings are held twice a year, in May and August, and the Cartmel Show takes place on the second Wednesday in August. Cartmel Priory, though, is the main attraction; established as an Augustinian priory in 1188, the church and a gatehouse have survived, the church with its two towers unusually set diagonally to each other and some surviving medieval glass, including John the Baptist and the Virgin and Child.

Cartmel Fell is a fascinating area of hills and hollows sprawling to the east of Lake Windermere, and is especially valuable as a quiet alternative to the overcrowded honeypots in summer. Amongst the centres of interest are the chapel, small and plain but an excellent example of its type and with a fine view (even better from the adjacent rocky, heathery knoll) over the sands of Morecambe Bay; the spinning galleries at Hodge Hill and Pool Bank; and the Mason's Arms, an extraordinary pub in a remote location on Strawberry Bank but with a mouth-watering selection of beers.

Castlerigg stone circle was described by Keats as 'a dismal cirque of Druid stones, upon a forlorn moor', but this was an unusually negative reaction to the sight of the Neolithic monument in its majestic mountain setting. Castlerigg is easily reached from Keswick and consequently is surprisingly popular; coach parties are amongst those making the journey back in time. There are 38 stones in a not-quite-perfect circle, with a further 10 stones set within the circle : the purpose of this extraordinary prehistoric construction is unknown. The views are stupendous and include Skiddaw, Blencathra – its southern ridges and gullies particularly well seen across the stone circle – the craggy north-western outliers of the Helvellyn massif, and the fells clustering around Grasmoor and Grisedale Pike.

Catbells is one of the most popular of the lower fells, being easily accessible from Keswick and very easily ascended on one of the broad paths which head for its summit. Perhaps the best plan is to ascend from Hawse End, south of the delectable gardens at Lingholm, then traverse the fell and descend from Hause Gate, the col separating Catbells and Maiden Moor, into Newlands at Little Town – taking care to avoid the mine workings in Yewthwaite Comb. The classic attribute of the fell is the tremendous prospect over Derwentwater, with its wooded islands, towards Keswick and, behind the town, the massive peaks of Skiddaw and Blencathra. On the eastern slopes of Catbells is Brandlehow Park, which was the first acquisition of the newly-formed National Trust in 1902. Further south, on the lower slopes, are the remains of the Brandlehow lead mine, together with Brackenburn, home of Sir Hugh Walpole, author of the Herries novels.

Chapel Stile functions now as one of the tourist centres of Great Langdale, but was previously populated mostly by workers in the slate quarries and the gunpowder works at Elterwater. The church dates from the middle of the nineteenth century; the curate in charge of its predecessor, only a century older, was recorded in 1787 as having to sell beer to keep body and soul together.

Cockermouth is a quietly attractive town with a long, broad main street. Although it is just outside the National Park it acts as a centre for much of the north-west quadrant of the Lake District. The ruined castle (open to the public on occasions) sits above an industrial quarter which includes Jennings Brewery; the castle dates from 1134 but little of the original structure, which was built partly from stones brought from the Roman fort of Derventio at nearby Papcastle, has survived. At the far end of the main street is the Georgian house which was William Wordsworth's birthplace. The house, which is now in the care of the National Trust, houses a small Wordsworth museum. The market at Cockermouth is a colourful and cheerful event; the first market charter dates from 1221 but it was not until 1638 that the Earl of Northumberland secured the right to hold a fair on summer Wednesdays.

Coniston, big village rather than small town, is the natural centre for walking in the Coniston Fells but otherwise is a little out of the mainstream. The village itself has tourist shops and a number of inns but is mainly a slate-grey former mining village, its prosperity founded in the ores of the Coppermines Valley, a short and instructive walk from Coniston alongside the Church Beck. Many walkers continue up to Levers Water, once a reservoir for the mines, and then climb up to the Old Man of Coniston, only just the highest of the Coniston Fells but with a tremendous southerly view. The village was once served by a particularly picturesque branch railway: built to transport copper and slate, it finally closed in 1957. Coniston Hall, just to the south of the village, is cruck-framed – a rarity hereabouts – and has tall cylindrical chimneys. In Coniston itself is the Ruskin Museum, well worth a visit for its collections of geological specimens, pictures and letters associated with John Ruskin.

Coniston Water is one of the most impressive of the lakes, with marvellous mountain scenery – especially effective when viewed from the east shore of the lake, near John Ruskin's home at Brantwood – and a good deal of public access, both by road at Monk Coniston and along the eastern shore, and by footpath as at Torver Back Common in the south-west. The lake is long, narrow and straight and as a result has been much favoured for world record water speed attempts, including the ill-fated trip of Donald Campbell in 1967. The steamboat *Gondola*, for some time a forlorn wreck at the southern end of the lake, has been restored and now offers a regular service. There is a boating centre and sailing club at Coniston Hall, and plenty of fishing. The lake, originally known as Thurston's Mere, was much used to export the ores from Coppermines Valley near Coniston, together with shipments of slate, and there are further signs of industry in the bloomery sites around its southern shores.

Crummock Water, 4km (2½ miles) long and almost 50m (160ft) deep, is the lower half of the massive post-glacial lake which once filled the flat valley floor of the Buttermere valley; deposition has created an alluvial plain separating it from Buttermere itself. Though there are attractive views across the lake to Grasmoor End, which rises precipitously above the bracken-infested common at Lanthwaite Green, Crummock Water is not one of the most picturesque lakes. Perhaps the best view of the lake itself is from the rough top of Rannerdale Knotts, which broods over the side valley containing the deserted medieval settlement of Rannerdale, whose chapel and farmhouses have vanished virtually without trace.

Dacre, though close to Ullswater, is off the beaten track but has much to offer the antiquarian. Most notable, perhaps, is its pele tower, built in the fourteenth century on the site of a Norman castle, restored somewhat later but still largely in its original condition. The castle can be approached via a public footpath but it is private property. The church of Dacre is also unusually interesting. The present building dates from the Norman period, as the sturdy west tower indicates, but it stands on the site of a Saxon monastery and there are Saxon remains to be discovered. In the churchyard are four strange stones, of unknown and mysterious origin.

Dale Head, the highest fell in the triangle of high land between Newlands Hause, Honister and Borrowdale, stands proudly at the head of the Newlands valley (hence the name) and there are tremendous views from its extremely attractive summit cairn. The fell is the focal point of the Newlands Round, an excellent fellwalking expedition, but can also be climbed from Honister Pass and (via Robinson) from Buttermere. Latterly there was considerable mining activity on the slopes of the mountain, and indeed the Dale Head copper mines below the summit, having been opened up by the German miners in the sixteenth century, were later developed by the Duke of Somerset, who built a bloomery at the site to process the ore. The ruined sheds and spoil heaps can still be seen; amongst the spoil are fragments with bright green copper malachite veins.

Derwentwater, close to Keswick and therefore extremely popular, is a wonderfully scenic lake which is just as breathtakingly beautiful when it fills the foreground as when it appears as the focal point of a distant view. Examples of the former are the well-known views along Borrowdale and across the lake to Causey Pike from Friar's Crag, and the sight of Blencathra across Derwentwater from near Brandlehow. More distant views of distinction include the very well-known shot from Ashness Bridge, on the road to Watendlath, with Derwentwater appearing in front of the green slopes of Skiddaw, and (a really wide-ranging and delightful view) Derwentwater and the green fields and woods of Borrowdale from the

Grains Gill route to Great End or from the striking summit cairn of Glaramara, a much underrated mountain. The lake itself, though 5km (3 miles) in length, is shallow, with a maximum depth of only 22m (72ft), and it is a good deal shallower than this in places, especially on the submarine ridges which run the length of the lake and at their highest form the islands which add so much to the charm of Derwentwater. St Herbert's Island, supposedly the hermitage of the eponymous saint, is the most southerly, while on Derwent Isle an eighteenth-century eccentric built a stone circle, church and fort.

Dunnerdale, the valley of the River Duddon, suffers in popularity because it has no lake and is somewhat inaccessible, but as a result its outstanding beauty can be savoured at leisure and in peace and quiet. Motorists are particularly well placed to seek out its attractions, for a good road follows the Duddon down from its source west of the Wrynose Pass to Cockley Beck and past Black Hall to Birks Bridge, a superb packhorse bridge high above a miniature gorge where the river flows through green pools between rock faces. Through Seathwaite, where there are stepping stones over the river, the road continues past woods and little rocky knolls to Ulpha, a hamlet with church and school where the Eskdale road rises steeply onto Birker Moor. Finally the Duddon reaches the sea near Broughton-in-Furness; the map indicates that the estuary of Duddon Sands, once famous for its salmon and cockles, is crossed by several tracks, but these are dangerous except to the experienced.

Egremont is a small town in the valley of the River Ehen south-east of Whitehaven, with a wide main street and the scanty remains of a Norman castle, constructed of St Bees sandstone around 1135 as a defence against incursions from the Scots. The gatehouse, with intricate herring-bone work, part of the Great Hall, and the outer walls and postern gate are the main survivals. Egremont owed its prosperity to iron ore, the first of its mines having been in existence by the late twelfth century (when it was presented as a gift to Holme Cultram Abbey). A highlight of the Egremont Crab Fair, held annually in September and a particularly boisterous event, is the World Championship Gurning Competition; gurning, of course, is the art of pulling a hideous face whilst wearing a horse collar.

Elterwater village, pleasantly situated at the entrance to Little Langdale, has an excellent pub and an attractive common popular for family picnics. To the north of the village is the site of the Elterwater gunpowder works, established in 1824 but closed a century later. The lake of Elterwater – literally 'swan lake' to the Norse settlers – is reedy, irregular and rather too small to capture the imagination; the waters of Great and Little Langdale (the Langdale Beck and River Brathay respectively) meet here.

Ennerdale Water is one of the most scenically pleasing of the lakes, though there will be many who have not had the pleasure of viewing it from, say, Kirkland, with the lake set between a foreground of meadowland and a distant view of mountains, with the jutting profile of Pillar Rock prominent on the higher slopes of its parent fell. From the site of the former Anglers' Hotel, unnecessarily demolished at a time when there were fears that the level of the lake would be raised to provide further water for west Cumberland, it is possible to follow the lake shore below Angler's Crag and along the southern side of the lake to its head near Gillerthwaite. Cars are not allowed as far as here: the car park below Bowness Knott is the limit for motorised traffic. A bridleway continues up the dale alongside the River Liza, however, passing through the much-criticised and extensive Forestry Commission plantations. It is a long walk to the head of Ennerdale, a truly remote spot with just the Black Sail Hut youth hostel amongst the sheep pastures, but the mountain scenery here is superb, with Great Gable, Pillar and Steeple outstanding.

Eskdale, though it contains no lake and, at least in its most frequented parts, is a little way distant from the major mountains, is nevertheless a favourite dale of many. It is certainly a dale of contrasts, beginning with the origins of the Esk itself high on the rock-strewn slopes dividing Esk Pike and Great End, two of the district's loftiest mountains. The infant Esk tumbles down into Great Moss, a wide flat bowl beneath Esk Buttress and the waterfall of Cam Spout, on the flanks of Scafell Pike and Scafell respectively. The site of a lake in late glacial times, Great Moss was later part of the monastic sheep pasture purchased by Furness Abbey in the thirteenth century; traces of the medieval boundary remain. Below Esk Falls and the packhorse bridge at Throstle Garth (where the monks' sheepfold survives) is the Norse farm of Brotherilkeld, now owned by the National Trust and the venue of the Eskdale Show in late September. The mid-valley, as far as Boot, offers superb riverside walks as the Esk passes under Doctor Bridge, dives through little gorges and ripples around the stepping stones next to St Catherine's chapel at Boot. Still lower down the valley the attractions include the Ravenglass & Eskdale narrow-gauge railway, Dalegarth Force in Stanley Ghyll, Muncaster Fell and, as the river nears the Irish Sea, Muncaster Castle and the village of Ravenglass, which overlooks the combined estuaries of the Esk, Irt and Mite.

Esthwaite Water, in its sylvan, gentle setting, presents a marked contrast to the rugged, brooding lakes which are often regarded as characteristic of the Lake District. From the south-east there is a fine view across the reedy, low-lying lake to the Langdale Pikes. Esthwaite Water, as befits a lowland lake in a farming area, supports a wide variety of fauna and flora, with trout, perch, pike, and roach amongst its fish. At the head of the lake, close to Hawkshead, is Priest Pot, a National Nature Reserve which was formerly part of Esthwaite Water but is now separated from the lake by an area of silty fen.

Fairfield is the centrepiece of a famous fell walk, the Fairfield Horseshoe, which is a popular and highly enjoyable excursion from Rydal or Ambleside. Fairfield itself is a mountain of contrasts, with smooth grassy slopes falling away into Rydale to the south, but rough scree, jagged rock precipices and tremendous deep, dark corries adorning the northern face of the fell and its immediate neighbours. So attractive is this northern aspect that Fairfield is best climbed from Patterdale, along Deepdale and under the towering crags of Greenhow End.

Glaramara, the highest of a complex series of fells dividing the upper reaches of Borrowdale from Langstrath, has an Old Norse name of obscure meaning, though part of the word appears to mean 'an abrupt descent or chasm', which could refer to the excellent hanging valley of Comb Gill below the summit to the north. Amongst the other features of the fell are the tremendous view north from its massive summit cairn along Borrowdale to Derwentwater and Skiddaw, and the strange (and somewhat dangerous) caves high on the side of the Comb Gill valley. The ridge walk from Glaramara to Allen Crags is delightful, with a number of tiny tarns forming perfect foregrounds for shots of the distant Langdale Pikes.

Glenridding, now to a large extent a place of hotels and tourist shops, was previously a mining village, its inhabitants dependent for their livelihood on the Greenside lead mine, which was so prosperous in the nineteenth century that the mining company owned more than fifty of the terraced houses in the village. The mine finally closed down in 1962, though by then it had had to survive some difficult times, notably when its reservoir (Keppelcove Tarn) broke its banks during a storm in 1927 and unleashed a torrent which destroyed bridges, buildings and livestock.

Gowbarrow Park is a particularly interesting area on the north-western shores of Ullswater. Originally a medieval deer park, Gowbarrow was planted in Victorian times with a variety of exotic trees, including Douglas fir and rhododendron, but it still retains its parkland atmosphere, with little rocky howes rising above the bracken. Aira Force, most romantic of Lakeland waterfalls, lies in the deeply incised valley of the Aira Beck; the water crashes down spectacularly into an enclosed, wooded ravine. The eighteenth-century hunting lodge of Lyulf's Tower, an extraordinary sight with its battlements, lies close to the shores of Ullswater here.

Grange-in-Borrowdale originated as the grange, or outlying farm, of Furness Abbey in the thirteenth century. Nowadays it is best known for its highly attractive bridge spanning the wide and shallow River Derwent. Just above the village are the Jaws of Borrowdale, where the valley becomes constricted and the river flows in a gorge between Castle Crag (its summit crowned by a hillfort) and Grange Fell, with the Bowder Stone, a glacial erratic, at its foot.

Grange-over-Sands, just outside the National Park, is a minor holiday resort with a promenade overlooking the muddy sands of Morecambe Bay. A highway crosses the sands from Kents Bank, near Grange, to the Lancashire coast, but the services of an experienced guide (appointed by the Duchy of Lancaster) are required by potential travellers, for knowledge of the tides, the river channels and the quicksands is essential. A fine viewpoint above the town is the little hill known as Hamps Fell, which has an area of limestone pavement on its summit.

Grasmere will need little introduction to many. Best visited outside the summer season or in the evening, after the crowds have dispersed, it is an attractive village which has come close to being overrun by commercial interests but still retains a measure of true charm. The tourists come here, of course, mainly to see Dove Cottage, though this is well to the east of the village centre, at Town End. Wordsworth's home for nine years during the period when his talent was at its height, it is open to the public, as is a nearby barn converted into a museum. The simple graves of the poet and his wife are in the churchyard at Grasmere, on a site chosen by Wordsworth and close to the yew trees he planted. St Oswald's church, its exterior hidden beneath an ashlar coat but with some thirteenth-century work inside, is the scene of an annual rushbearing ceremony which originated because until the nineteenth century the floor of the church was composed of bare earth and was strewn with rushes. The lake of Grasmere is some distance from the village but is easily approached on foot; the best view is from Loughrigg Terrace at the southern end. Grasmere sports, held on the Thursday closest to 20 August, are the biggest in the district, and include hound trailing, Cumberland wrestling and pole jumping as well as the Guides Race, one of the most famous of all the fell races.

Grasmoor is the highest of the north-western fells, but does not often get the credit it deserves, largely because a number of the nearby peaks, such as Grisedale Pike, are rather more shapely. Nevertheless its western face, Grasmoor End, towers commandingly above Crummock Water, and the direct ascent from Lanthwaite Green is an unremittingly hard slog on unstable scree and over bilberries and heathery rock outcrops. The summit is disappointing, consisting of a broad grassy plateau, though there is evidence of periglacial activity in the stone polygons and stone stripes which can appear after hard frosts. There is an extensive view from the summit across the blue waters of Buttermere, Crummock Water and Loweswater to the High Stile range, with Helvellyn and the Scafell range amongst the more distant peaks. The northern face of Grasmoor drops steeply over Dove Crags into the stony wastes of Gasgale Gill – an abrupt transformation from the grassy summit scenes.

Great Gable, the fell chosen to be the symbol of the National Park, is best seen from Wasdale or from Lingmell, where the magnificent crags forming the Great Napes are displayed to full advantage. The best, though certainly not the easiest, way to the top also starts from Wasdale, ascending the ridge of Gavel Neese to the projecting rock known as Moses' Finger, then using the climbers' traverse under the Great Napes, scrambling up the scree shoot of Great Hell Gate and around the edge of Westmorland Crags, and finally traversing a bouldery plateau to the summit cairn and the nearby war memorial of the Fell and Rock Climbing Club. Amongst the astonishing, complex rock scenery of the Great Napes is the Napes Needle, scene of Walter Parry Haskett-Smith's momentous rock climb in 1886, while on the northern face of the mountain is the great black wall of Gable Crag. A cave high on the crag was reputedly the refuge of Moses, a legendary whisky smuggler, whose route through the fells – Moses' Trod – can still be followed from Honister round the head of Ennerdale and across the slopes of Great Gable to Wasdale Head.

Great Langdale is one of the most popular of Lakeland valleys, with a wealth of interest from Elterwater to the head of the dale in the wild recesses of Mickleden and Oxendale. The Langdale Pikes dominate the views up-valley, and they are usually climbed from the path starting behind the New Dungeon Ghyll Hotel. Stickle Tarn and Pavey Ark increase the scenic quality of this walk. The Old

Dungeon Ghyll Hotel is the base for more serious expeditions by walkers bound for the majestic fells at the head of the valley – notably Bowfell – or for the Scafell range, and by rock climbers making for Gimmer and other major crags. High on the flanks of Pike o' Stickle is the site of a Neolithic stone axe factory, the most important in the country. Amongst the other fells making up the impressive skyline at the head of the dale are Pike of Blisco and Crinkle Crags; a marvellous ridge walk connects the two.

Grizedale Forest, acquired by the Forestry Commission in 1934, has been developed with the interests of forestry, amenity and recreation in mind, and in addition to the usual hardwood plantations it includes oak coppice woodland and open areas of fell and farmland. Areas of larch have been planted to allow the red deer, for which the area is renowned, to remain. The visitor centre, to the north of Satterthwaite, includes a wildlife museum, information centre, a nature trail and, in a converted barn, the Theatre in the Forest.

Hardknott is a low fell which lends its name to the Hardknott Pass, the steepest and most tortuous of the drivers' routes in the district yet one which was used by the Romans for their road between the forts of Galava (Ambleside) and Glannaventa (Ravenglass). The substantial remains of the Roman fort at Hardknott, on a shoulder of the fell overlooking the delightful scenery of the Esk valley and also blessed with an outstanding view of the Scafell range across upper Eskdale, are outstanding and well worth the effort required to bring them underfoot. The walls, carefully restored by the Department of the Environment, still stand to a height of several feet, and the four gateways – one facing out directly onto a steep drop into Eskdale and therefore serving no practical purpose – are very much in evidence, together with the principal buildings both inside the fort and, a little to the south, around the bath-house. Some distance to the east is a level area, with a raised viewing platform, which was the Roman parade ground.

Hartsop, strictly speaking Low Hartsop, is best known for the exterior spinning galleries which decorate a number of the farmhouses in the hamlet. The galleries, dating from the seventeenth century, were the open platforms where local wool was spun before being sent to the woollen mills of Keswick, Kendal and elsewhere, and their survival preserves the evidence of a localised but important architectural tradition. Hartsop is also a good starting point for the exploration of the High Street ridge and for routes to Thornthwaite Crag, with its impressive summit monolith.

Haweswater reservoir, created in the 1930s to supply water to Manchester, at the cost of drowning the hamlet of Mardale Green and its venerable church, inn and farmhouses, is nobody's favourite. The ugly tidemark around the shoreline and the unattractive marshes at its head see to that, though there are some fine views across the reservoir to the High Street range. In times of drought the buildings of Mardale Green can still be seen.

Hawkshead, though it has lost some of its former importance and can now claim only village status, has much to offer the visitor. Clues to its more illustrious past include the church with its massive tower, a legacy of Hawkshead's days as a wool town, and Hawkshead Court House, a little outside the village, which was the grange farm of Furness Abbey during the monks' ascendancy in Furness. The centres of attraction now are the two squares, linked by a narrow alley, and the cobbled lanes and courtyards lined in some cases by overhanging buildings dating from the great rebuilding in the seventeenth century. Hawkshead Grammar School was where William Wordsworth was educated, and the school has been maintained much as he would have known it, with the original desks and benches. Above all the village should be visited for the views of the fells from the town, and especially from the churchyard.

Helvellyn has the reputation of being the most popular mountain in the Lake District, largely because of its accessibility from Grasmere and Patterdale rather than the intrinsic attractiveness of its summit or its western approaches. Its eastern face, however, is very different, with the two celebrated, narrow and rocky aretes of Striding Edge and Swirral Edge separated by a deep corrie containing Red Tarn. Though Striding Edge can be dangerous in wintry conditions it is so popular that help is never far away, and it is undoubtedly an exhilarating way to the top of the mountain. At 950m (3,118ft) Helvellyn is one of the four Lakeland Threethousanders, but its summit is cluttered with cairns, most of them unnecessary, as well as shelters, a triangulation column and even two memorials – one commemorating a dog which stayed with its dead master in 1855 and another the landing of an aeroplane on the flat summit ridge some seventy years later. Of the fourteen routes which converge on its summit the most celebrated is undoubtedly that over Striding Edge, though the route over Catstycam and Swirral Edge is almost as exciting.

Hesket Newmarket, nowadays a quietly attractive village, was (as its name implies) once a reasonably prosperous market town, as evidenced by the extremely large central green with a surviving market cross. Sheep and cattle fairs were held here until the early years of the nineteenth century, but the village was too far off the beaten track to sustain them in the railway age. Now the long village green provides the focus for a series of attractive limestone cottages and farmhouses; nearby Hesket Hall is more unusual architecturally, cube-shaped and with a circular roof.

High Street is both the highest point of the most easterly of the Lake District's main ridges and also the name of a Roman road which, somewhat improbably, traverses the same range of fells. The ridge is long and generally composed of smooth, grassy slopes, though there are impressive crags above Blea Water and a fine ridge rises from Mardale Head to the summit plateau; the summit itself is of no great interest. The Roman road is still traceable in its entirety, coming up from the narrow Straits of Riggindale and passing to the west of the summit on its way to the Trout Beck valley. The Mardale shepherds' meet was held annually on the summit plateau until 1835, with barrels of beer rolled up from the dale and wrestling and horse-racing amongst the attractions (hence the alternative name of Racecourse Hill).

The green village of Hesket Newmarket, on the northern fringes of the Lake District. The eighteenth-century market cross, with four round pillars supporting a pyramid roof, is the only reminder of busier times at this failed market town

Honister Pass carries the road from Seatoller in Borrowdale to Buttermere and is especially picturesque as it descends Gatesgarthdale into the latter valley, with the crags of the High Stile fells prominently in view. At the top of the pass are buildings associated with Honister Quarries, which have been producing high-quality slate since at least 1634 and are still operating. The old toll road from Honister to Seatoller offers a pleasant alternative to the motor road for walkers, whilst those in pursuit of something more strenuous can tackle Dale Head, or follow the ridge southwards to Great Gable.

Ill Bell (Kentmere) is the central peak in a quite delightful little ridge which separates upper Kentmere from the Trout Beck valley. The lesser peaks are Froswick, to the north – from where the ridge goes on to link up with the High Street fells – and Yoke, better known for its craggy eastern slopes, culminating in Rainsborrow Crag. Ill Bell has a knobbly, corrugated summit plateau festooned with cairns, and makes an attractive destination from Troutbeck, though devious routes via the Garburn Road and Yoke, or Scot Rake (used by the Romans as part of their road from Penrith along the High Street ridge to Ambleside) and Froswick, are preferable to the unremitting toil of a direct ascent.

Ireby was once a market town of some little pretension but no longer functions as such; the Thursday market and the annual fair, granted in 1237, were still flourishing more than four centuries later but have long since been abandoned.

The butter cross and Moot Hall are now private houses and they, together with the market place, remain as reminders of the village's former importance. Ireby old church, some distance to the west, is a disused Norman chapel, and another deserted site in the vicinity is that of the Iron Age settlement at Aughertree.

Irton parish must be one of the most dispersed in the Lake District. The church stands alone on a slight hill commanding a good view of the Wasdale fells; in the churchyard is an excellent Anglian cross. Also in the parish is the hamlet of Santon Bridge, while Irton Fell is the first summit in the long ridge of Whin Rigg and Illgill Head, best known for its north-west slopes, which form the Wastwater Screes, the famous backdrop to the district's deepest and most forbidding lake.

Kendal caters largely for the tourist nowadays, though it still has an important market and administrative function. The ruined castle, sited on a drumlin (a mound of glacial boulder clay) across the Kent valley, and the burgage plots, alleys and courtyards in the streets around the market place are the most significant reminders of its medieval functions, while the disused canal and the adjacent industrial quarter testify to its later growth. The parish church, Holy Trinity, has five aisles together with chapels to three local families, including the Parrs – Catherine Parr, who became the sixth wife of Henry VIII in 1543, was born in Kendal castle. There is an art gallery and museum at Abbot Hall, near the church, an annual festival of music and, in September, the Westmorland County Show.

Kentmere is the name of a hamlet, a dale, a reservoir and a minor fell, Kentmere Pike. The hamlet consists of a heavily restored church with a grey ashlared tower, Kentmere Hall – an amalgam of fourteenth-century pele tower and later farmhouse – and a cluster of farmhouses and cottages above the River Kent. There is no pub: in a notorious case in the nineteenth century the Low Bridge Inn (now a private house) became the first pub in England to lose its licence as a result of drunkenness and immorality. The dale, of which the hamlet is the focal point, is chiefly notable for the diatomite works which processes the clay from the bed of the former valley lake. The reservoir, in an attractive mountain setting, was built to regulate the flow of water to the mills much further down the Kent valley. Above the reservoir the old packhorse route from Kentmere to Mardale can be seen ascending the delightful though very steep Nan Bield Pass.

Keswick is much-maligned, but though it does suffer from the excesses of tourism it retains a good deal of character and interest. It began life late, obtaining its first market charter in the closing years of the thirteenth century and growing as a centre for miners from Newlands and Borrowdale and later as a woollen town. Now it functions purely as a tourist centre. The Moot Hall dates from 1813 and is now the information centre; Greta Hall is notable as the home for 40 years of the poet Robert Southey; and there are a number of alleyways, such as Packhorse Yard and Woolpack Yard, running down to the River Greta from the main street. In King's Head Yard, Jonathon Otley, clockmaker turned amateur but gifted geologist, had his home. In Fitz Park is a small art gallery and museum, which contains manuscripts of the Lake poets, a scale model of the Lake District, and strange 'musical stones' which were played at Buckingham Palace in 1848.

Little Langdale suffers in comparison with its bigger brother but is justifiably popular with many; the road through the dale is far *too* popular in summer, congested with motorists travelling over the Wrynose Pass, with its twisting bends and steep gradients, or visiting Blea Tarn in its idyllic location on a shelf between the two Langdales. The hamlet of Little Langdale is tiny, with just a pub, a school and a few cottages, but a lane on the left here leads to Slater Bridge, a marvellous bridge approached by a flagstoned causeway and spanning the Brathay on huge slate slabs. Originally built by quarrymen needing to reach their work in the Wetherlam quarries, the bridge now caters for walkers bound for the Coniston Fells or Colwith Force. Little Langdale Tarn is a disappointing and rather inaccessible sheet of water by Lake District standards. Behind Fell Foot Farm, owned by the National Trust, is a strange mound which might be a Viking 'thing-mount' or meeting place.

Longsleddale is a fascinating dale which, by virtue of its peripheral location, is usually comparatively quiet. The dale head, above the picturesque hamlet of Sadgill, with its classically simple packhorse bridge over the turbulent River Sprint, is wild and rugged, with the Gatescarth Pass carrying an old trade route over to Mardale. Lower down the pele tower of Ubarrow Hall is the focus of interest. There are now no lakes in the dale, though the sites of a number which clearly existed in the immediate post-glacial period can be discerned without too much difficulty.

Lorton consists of two settlements, High and Low, which together make up a village of considerable interest. There was once a good deal of industry here, based on water power from the River Cocker, and indeed the surviving Cockermouth brewery, Jennings, originated in the village; the village hall is on the site of the former maltings. Lorton Hall is a complex building of some interest, with traces of a fifteenth-century pele tower, further medieval fragments, and seventeenth-century additions incorporated in the present structure. The hall is said to be haunted by a woman carrying a lighted candle, and it has seen a variety of royal visitors, including Malcolm III of Scotland in the eleventh century and Charles II in 1653.

Loweswater, tucked away in a side valley with its outflow quickly swallowed up in Crummock Water, is a lovely little lake perhaps best approached from the roadside on its northern shore, though a relatively lightly used footpath threads its way through woodland on the opposite shore and is perhaps a pleasanter way to get to know the lake. Loweswater enjoys a close relationship with Mellbreak, a fell with dramatic crags and fine views despite its lack of height. The 'village' of Loweswater, loosely centred on the church and the Kirkstile Inn, is very scattered but supports the Loweswater Show and a vintage car rally in the autumn.

Lowther estate is now best known as a country park with adventure playgrounds, assault course, jousting tournaments and the like, and the castle is a mere shell. Yet there has been a castle here since the thirteenth century, and the estate has been in the hands of the Lowthers during all that period. The ruined facade which is all that is left of the castle is a much more recent rebuilding, however, having

The imposing facade of Lowther Castle seen from the Celleron road

been constructed in 1806-11 to the plans of Robert Smirke, architect of the British Museum. The church of St Michael is the sole survivor of the former village of Lowther, its houses pulled down in the late seventeenth century by Sir John Lowther 'to enlarge his demesne, and open the prospect of his house, for they stood just in front of it'. Earthworks near the church indicate the former village street and the house sites. The villagers were relocated at Newtown, an estate village begun in 1683 which also housed a carpet factory. The church has a Victorian tower but an early medieval interior, and there is a strange Lowther family mausoleum in the churchyard.

Mardale retains a great deal of its appeal despite the intrusion of Haweswater reservoir in the 1930s, with the consequent loss of the delightful small village of Mardale Green. The dalehead is ringed with fine mountains, including Harter Fell with its forbidding, craggy northern face and High Street, the highest of these eastern fells. A number of excellent walks start from the car park at Mardale Head, notably those over the Gatescarth Pass to Longsleddale and the exquisite Nan Bield Pass to Kentmere, and up the long narrow ridge of Rough Crag and Long Stile to High Street. The Nan Bield route passes Small Water, one of the very best of the district's tarns, with a number of peculiar low wall shelters close to the water's edge, and runs below the corrie containing Blea Water, the deepest Lakeland tarn. An alternative walk, also of considerable historic interest, is to follow the Old Corpse Road eastwards from Mardale over Selside End to Swindale and Shap.

Martindale is a secluded side valley on the eastern side of Ullswater, and also gives its name to a large area of common, much of it inaccessible to the public and the home since medieval times of an important herd of red deer. There are two churches in Martindale: the newer one, extravagantly Victorian but of no great architectural interest, is the starting point for the easy walk to the summit of Hallin Fell, but the older dale chapel is worth seeing. There was a chapel here in the fourteenth century, but the present simple structure, nave and chancel all in one, dates from 1633.

Moor Divock, a hive of prehistoric activity, is now an excellent spot for picnics or for easy walks along the wide grassy tracks – one of them on the line of the Roman road from Brocavum, near Penrith, to Galava (Ambleside). Amongst the many prehistoric survivals are The Cockpit, by far the best preserved of seven stone circles identified in the vicinity, with 65 stones and a diameter of 36m (120ft); an unusual and rather impressive cairn circle; and the Cop Stone, a single remnant of yet another stone circle. There are many more burial mounds, and a variety of minor hills and hollows which are in many cases unexplained.

Muncaster Castle occupies an outstanding position in the lower Esk valley, with Muncaster Fell immediately behind and the blue line of the Scafell range in the distance. The house itself is essentially a Victorian country house tacked onto a pre-existing pele tower (dating from about 1325), with a second matching pele tower dating only from the 1860s. Owned by the Pennington family since the thirteenth century, the castle is open to the public and perhaps most notable for its collection of antique furniture. The grounds are a delight, with a superb array of landscaped gardens, including the Terrace Walk, ingeniously developed on the delta terrace of the glacial Lake Eskdale, and a collection of rhododendrons which is amongst the finest in Europe.

Mungrisdale is one of the classic moorland hamlets of Back o' Skidda' country, on the very edge of the fells and overlooking the eerie plains stretching eastward towards Greystoke. Its whitewashed cottages and solid farmsteads are loosely clustered around the tiny church of St Kentigern, also known as St Mungo (hence the placename). The church, with nave and chancel in one, dates from 1756 and has a three-decker pulpit and a 1617 Bible in a glass case. Above the River Glenderamackin stands the Mill Inn, traditional focal point of one of the most celebrated shepherds' meets.

Newby Bridge was clearly once at the extreme southern end of Windermere, since there is a complex series of end moraines here indicating the point at which the Windermere glacier rested for a while and deposited its debris. Now, however, the site of the village lies some distance from the lake, although a steam railway (the Lakeside and Haverthwaite Railway) connects village and lake. Tourism is the mainstay here, given the village's location at the junction of A590 and A592.

Newlands is a quite magnificent valley, deep, straight and heavily glaciated, and ringed by a number of fine fells, none better than Dale Head, so named because of its position closing the valley head. The valley was the focus of the pioneering

The church and adjacent former schoolhouse at Little Town in the Newlands valley

mining exploits of the Society for the Mines Royal in the sixteenth century, and mine ruins or spoil heaps can still be seen high on the flanks of Dale Head and at Castle Nook and Goldscope. The focus of present-day settlement is the hamlet of Little Town and the nearby dale chapel, idyllically situated with Catbells as a green backcloth. Next to the chapel is the tiny building which formerly housed the school.

Nether Wasdale, also known as Strands, is nothing more than a collection of farms, cottages and inns in the Irt valley below the outflow from Wastwater. There is a chapel with carvings from York Minster and ornate ceiling and panelling, but nothing else of great note except the scenery, which is stunning, especially from slightly higher ground on one of the many footpaths which lie close at hand. A particularly rewarding route lies across Irton Fell to Eskdale; another runs past Easthwaite to the foot of Wastwater; and yet another makes for the base of the crags at Buckbarrow, with excellent views of Great Gable and the Scafell range.

Old Man of Coniston. The Old Man, though it is only 803m (2,631ft) high – and indeed overtops the next highest peak in the Coniston Fells, Swirl How, by a mere 30cm (1ft) – has a special place in the affections of fellwalkers, and as a consequence its higher reaches are rarely deserted. The summit, though part of a broad plateau, is perched above steep slopes overlooking the corrie tarn of Low

Water, and has a substantial cairn, wall shelter and OS column. The view along Coniston Water and over the estuaries feeding into Morecambe Bay is stunning. Closer at hand are the marvellous, complex rock buttresses of Dow Crag across the wild upland tarn of Goat's Water. On the flanks of the fell are extensive mine workings, particularly but not exclusively in Coppermines Valley; another of the Old Man's tarns, Levers Water, was enlarged to serve as a reservoir for the mines.

Patterdale is a village of no great interest which has one priceless asset, namely its magnificent setting at the head of Ullswater, with a series of delightful fells at hand. Notable is Place Fell, quite easily climbed and with a marvellous view over Ullswater to the Helvellyn range. Helvellyn itself is the most popular destination by far for walkers from Patterdale, with the main route to the mountain, via the famous arete of Striding Edge, heading up Grisedale. Patterdale was described by H. H. Symonds in 1933, in *Walking in the Lake District*, as 'a most unlovely place, made of buses and booths and scrappy bits of architectural jumble', and few would quarrel with those sentiments today. St Patrick's Well, in a gabled recess by the roadside north of the village, supposedly had healing properties; the medieval chapel dedicated to him was rebuilt in 1853. The main event of the year is the sheepdog trials, held on the last Saturday in August.

Penrith is a fine medieval market town, sometimes very busy as locals and tourists jostle in the shopping streets but worth attention for its red sandstone castle, much extended by Richard III in a forlorn attempt to deter Scots border raiders, its church with thick tower walls dating from the Norman period but otherwise much altered in the eighteenth century, and its churchyard with a collection of Viking hogback tombstones and pre-Norman churchyard crosses. There is a fine array of market places, including the site of the old cattle fairs at Great Dockray and the stock market in Sandgate. Near the centrally-situated churchyard is the former Queen Elizabeth Grammar School, a fine sandstone building which housed the school, founded in 1564, until 1915. The Town Hall is an adaptation of two town houses attributed to Robert Adam.

Pillar is an impressive mountain with an even more impressive feature on its northern flanks, namely Pillar Rock, an extravagant outcrop thrusting up some 150m (500ft) from the Ennerdale slopes of the fell and comprising a series of buttresses and gullies peppered with excessively difficult and exposed rock climbs, but providing spectators (notably those camped at Robinson's Cairn on the High Level Route to the summit of the mountain) with exceptional mountain scenery uncommonly close at hand. First climbed in 1826 by a local shepherd, John Atkinson, the Rock has had its devotees ever since, and John Wilson Robinson, after whom Robinson's Cairn is named, made more than a hundred ascents after first scaling Pillar Rock in 1882. The summit of Pillar is surprisingly gentle and grassy after all this rock splendour, with numerous cairns and a ruined fence amongst the artefacts. Though the High Level Route is the most exciting way to the top, purists will probably insist on climbing Pillar from Ennerdale, though this involves a long walk up the dale (and just as long a return late in the day!).

Pooley Bridge is a fairly sizeable and quite pretty village sited at the northern tip of

Ullswater, where the River Eamont begins its journey to the Eden valley. This was a former market centre, with a fish market and September sheep and cattle fair in the nineteenth century, and the site of the former market place is still betrayed by a bulge in the road in the centre of the village. Dunmallet Hill, overlooking the village, is a rounded hill surmounted by a hillfort, probably of Iron Age date, where stone axes have been discovered. There is fishing and boating on Ullswater, and a steamer service along the lake, calling at Howtown and Glenridding Pier. The best short drive is that along the eastern side of the lake to Howtown and Martindale; the best short walk heads east to Moor Divock, with its prehistoric remains and excellent views of Ullswater, the Helvellyn fells and, well to the east, the long escarpment of the Pennines.

Portinscale, west of Keswick and near the exquisite Lingholm Gardens, and with the road to Newlands and along the west bank of Derwentwater to Grange threading its way through the village, is surprisingly unpretentious, though it caters for tourism and particularly for sailing enthusiasts. The placename, inexplicably, is derived fron the old Norse for 'the prostitute's dwelling'.

Ravenglass, nowadays a quiet village sited at the water's edge, has had a long and varied past, starting with the arrival of the Romans, whose fort (Glannaventa) is nowadays best represented by the bath-house known as Walls Castle. In medieval times efforts were made to promote the growth of Ravenglass into a fully-fledged market town, but these efforts foundered and although there are clues to be found in the wide main street, the annual fair is nowadays just a tourist attraction. Another magnet for the tourists is the Ravenglass & Eskdale narrow-gauge railway, originally a mineral line serving the iron ore mines near Boot but converted for passenger use and now a very pleasant way to travel up the lower Esk valley. Across the estuary from Ravenglass is the Drigg Dunes nature reserve.

Red Pike (Buttermere) is a very popular mountain, often climbed from Buttermere village and easily recognised in views from across the valley because of the gash of red scree below its summit. Together with High Stile and High Crag it offers an exciting ridge walk between the Buttermere and Ennerdale valleys. The red scree exists because most of the fell is composed of an igneous intrusion, the Ennerdale granophyre. A notable element in the landscape is Bleaberry Tarn, couched in a deep corrie between Red Pike and High Stile. Robert Southey once described it as the crater of an extinct volcano, but it is of course glacial in origin. The stream issuing from Bleaberry Tarn cascades over the lip of the corrie as a foaming torrent after heavy rain; this Sour Milk Gill deserves its name, and is capable of heavy destruction of the stream bed in winter.

Red Pike (Wasdale) presents a bold face to the hamlet of Wasdale Head; its crags thrust upwards above reddish scree slopes cascading down into the U-shaped trough of Mosedale. The higher slopes are very pleasant, consisting of a long ridge with rocky promontories culminating in a summit perched above the crags. Scoat Tarn, in a green hollow to the left, and the familiar outlines of Scafell Pike and Scafell, separated by the col of Mickledore, are prominent features of the view from The Chair, a belvedere cunningly constructed around a rock outcrop south of the summit. Red Pike is a major goal on the Mosedale Horseshoe, one of the finest ridge walks in the Lake District, and highly scenic ridges connect it to its neighbours, Pillar and Yewbarrow.

Rosthwaite is a tiny village in Borrowdale, outstandingly well placed for walkers, who can choose between serious expeditions at the head of Borrowdale and gentler excursions through the Stonethwaite valley to Grasmere, along Langstrath to Langdale, or across Grange Fell to the unspoilt hamlet of Watendlath. The village itself, sited on The How, a rocky knoll above the flat valley floor of the River Derwent, which is liable to flood hereabouts, has inns, a shop and a number of pleasant stone cottages.

Rydal, an attractive little settlement in its own right, owes its fame to its Wordsworth connection. The poet lived almost half his life at Rydal Mount, from 1813 to 1850, and the house is inundated with summer visitors, who come to see the period furniture and the garden, laid out as Wordsworth knew it. They also come to see Dora's Field, behind Rydal church (an unprepossessing edifice dating from 1824); the field still sports a host of daffodils in spring, and is carefully tended by the National Trust. Rydal Hall, along the lane from the poet's house, is mainly

The combined estuaries of Irt, Mite and Esk at Ravenglass, looking towards the Drigg Dunes gullery and nature reserve

of the seventeenth century though with Victorian additions; the Park is the venue for Rydal sheepdog trials in August.

Rydal Water is the smallest of the lakes and has a maximum depth of only about 18m (60ft). Nevertheless, it is attractive and accessible, and it is relatively easy for lakeshore walkers to escape the busy A591 by taking a footpath leading around the southern shores of the lake onto the lower slopes of Loughrigg Fell. At the eastern end of the lake stone steps lead up a rocky knoll to Wordsworth's Seat, reportedly the great man's most loved viewpoint. To see the lake in its wider setting a walk along Sweden Bridge Lane from Ambleside is highly recommended.

St John's in the Vale has a number of features of interest, notably the view of Blencathra from its southern end, the Castle Rock of Triermain – now a noted haunt of rock climbers, but also the setting for Sir Walter Scott's *The Bridal of Triermain* and reputedly the site of the Green Chapel in the medieval poem *Sir Gawayne and the Green Knight* – and the finely situated dale chapel on the northern shoulder of High Rigg, to the west of St John's Beck.

Sawrey consists of two settlements, Near and Far. Far Sawrey, closest to the Windermere ferry, is unremarkable, but at Near Sawrey is Hill Top Farm. This was the home of Beatrix Potter, and the surrounding countryside clearly

influenced the 'Peter Rabbit' series of children's books which she wrote and illustrated. The house, with its attractive and carefully preserved interior, is open from Easter to November, and is in the ownership of the National Trust, as is the adjacent and very comfortable pub, the Tower Bank Arms, which makes a guest appearance in *The Tale of Jemima Puddleduck.*

Scafell is the second highest mountain in England, but though it is physically very close to the highest, Scafell Pike, it is separated from it by the dramatic col of Mickledore, and there is no direct route for walkers between the two summits. The summit of Scafell is set on a fairly level plateau, and there are few items of interest in the near vicinity: the highest point is marked only by a cairn of no great distinction and Foxes Tarn, second highest in the Lake District, is only a small pool. The great glory of Scafell, however, is the tremendous cliff of naked rock on its northern face. Scafell Crag, scene of many of the early advances in the sport of rock climbing, and the lower Shamrock Buttress combine to provide an overwhelming sight. Between the two the rocky, slippery, steep gully known as Lord's Rake, the most famous scramblers' route in the district, makes its way from the scree-laden bowl of Hollow Stones to the summit plateau. On the east and south-east there are still further crags, with Esk Buttress and Cam Spout Crag (the latter containing the waterfall of Cam Spout) dropping dramatically to the desolate upper Esk valley.

Scafell Pike, the highest land in England, has few of the subtleties of fells which may be of lesser height but can claim far greater beauty. Its summit plateau is an uncompromisingly barren mass of boulders and the summit itself, though inevitably very popular, has nothing more than a massive but derelict wallshelter for a cairn. As befits its status, it has a very wide view over the surrounding fells and westwards to the Irish Sea. The shortest route to the summit starts at Wasdale Head and climbs alongside the Lingmell Gill; better but longer alternatives come up from Borrowdale, along the Corridor Route, and from Langdale via Esk Hause and the shoulder of Great End; but surely the best of all starts at Brotherilkeld and traverses upper Eskdale before climbing the little known peak of Pen and reaching the summit plateau up the enclosed gully of Little Narrowcove.

Seathwaite, the only settlement of any real note in the Duddon valley (Dunnerdale), is a hamlet with farm cottages, a pub and a church which, whilst it has been over-restored, is still notable for one of its former curates, 'Wonderful Walker', made famous by his inclusion in Wordsworth's poem *The Excursion.* Nicholas Walker was curate here for 66 years, and also filled the jobs of farm labourer, teacher, and nurse as well as spinning wool and making clothes for his family.

Shap, between Penrith and Kendal, is a rugged village perched high on the bleak and inhospitable Shap Fell, that curse of travellers along the A6, main railway and, more recently and less noticeably, the M6. Shap is, of course, best known for its granite quarries, though these are some distance to the south of the village. There is a considerable continuity of settlement in the area, with standing stones, cairns and the scanty remains of a stone circle (much of it destoyed by the building

Shap Abbey

of the railway) in the vicinity. To the west are the substantial remains of Shap Abbey in the quiet valley of the River Lowther; the abbey was founded in 1150, but the massive tower was completed only just before the dissolution in 1540, and it forms the major survival.

Skiddaw, at 931m (3,053ft) the least elevated of the four Lakeland Threethousanders (fells of 3,000ft or more), is also the easiest to climb, with bulky slopes running down southwards towards Keswick and eastwards to Skiddaw House. The tourist route over Latrigg and Jenkin Hill is very easy to follow and in truth a little tedious, though it does have the merit of including the outstanding viewpoint of Skiddaw Little Man, with its magnificent views along Borrowdale to the central fells. More exciting routes can be devised to the north and west, with Ullock Pike and Carl Side very worthwhile objectives. Skiddaw House was once a shepherd's cottage of exceptional remoteness, but is now a youth hostel. Skiddaw Forest is a vast, bare and lonely area of spongy grassland and heather moorland which in medieval times was reserved as hunting country.

Staveley is a large and somewhat nondescript village which lies astride the busy Kendal to Windermere road. At one time it was a minor market centre, with a charter granted in 1329, but Kendal gradually usurped its trade. Later the village became a focal point for the bobbin industry of the southern Lake District, with five mills in the Kent and Gowan valleys in the mid-nineteenth century. A minor road from Staveley follows the River Kent upstream past the diatomite works near Millrigg to the hamlet of Kentmere.

Stonethwaite is a delightful hamlet in the side valley of the same name near Rosthwaite in Borrowdale. The classic view of the Stonethwaite valley is indeed from the road between Rosthwaite and Seatoller, with the notably steep and rocky western face of Eagle Crag closing the view up the valley. The two streams contributing to the Stonethwaite Beck are the Langstrath Beck and Greenup Gill; at their confluence is Smithymire Island, where the monks of Fountains Abbey smelted iron ore at a primitive bloomery. An ancient packhorse route runs along Stonethwaite and over Greenup Edge, connecting Borrowdale and Grasmere.

Sty Head, on the walkers' route between Wasdale and Borrowdale and an intermediate objective of routes to Scafell Pike and Great Gable, soon becomes familiar to regular walkers in the Lake District. So important a route is it that there was a proposal to drive a motor road over the Sty Head Pass in the late nineteenth century; fortunately this was successfully resisted. Sty Head Tarn has a reedy shoreline which indicates that it was once much larger.

Swinside is the name of a wooded hill and hamlet in the lower reaches of the Newlands valley. The hill is prominent in views from the fells making up the Newlands round; from Dale Head it appears as a dark green shadow in front of the bulky Skiddaw. The hamlet consists of little more than a farm and an excellent inn on the road from Portinscale to Stair and, across Newlands Hause, Buttermere.

Tarn Hows, artificially created in the nineteenth century by damming a stream passing through a marshy valley, is now one of the most famous and popular tourist destinations in the country, and few regular visitors to the Lake District will have been able to resist the temptation to include the easy walk around the tarn in their itinerary. The car parks are expensive but usually full, and the pressure on the paths is such that repair work is constantly needed to combat the problems of erosion. The tarn itself is picturesque, but it comes into its own as a foreground for marvellous views of both the Helvellyn range and the Langdale Pikes.

Thirlmere has belonged since 1879 to the Manchester Corporation Water Works, and its water, suitably treated south of Dunmail Raise, still travels 150km (95 miles) south to meet the needs of Manchester. Most of the catchment area is forested, though there are still some tenanted farms, and it is only within the last few years that proposals for public access and improvement of what was once an unimaginatively planted landscape have come to the fore. Some 2,000 acres have been planted with conifers since 1908. By far the best plan for those wishing to see the reservoir at its best is to take the road along the west shore, from where there are a number of access points, together with forest trails at Launchy Gill and a number of footpaths across to Watendlath.

Thornthwaite Forest occupies much of the low fell country on either side of the Whinlatter Pass, the relatively easy pass between Lorton and Braithwaite, and although much of the planting pays little attention to the landscape – as in the blocks of conifers below Grisedale Pike and Hopegill Head – there are encouraging signs that the Forestry Commission is mending its ways and seizing the opportunity provided by clear felling to enhance the landscape with its planting. The forest also includes outliers such as Dodd, the little fell on the side of Skiddaw, where there is an excellent forest walk. At the summit of the Whinlatter Pass there is a very good visitor centre with displays, audio-visual presentations and bookshop inside and forest trails and picnic areas outside.

Threlkeld is a large village, formerly dependent on the mines nearby at Gategill and Woodend and still concerned with quarrying, between Keswick and Penrith. As such it is well situated for exploration of the northern fells and has easy access to central Lakeland, yet it is far from overrun by tourists. The former open field, covering 14 acres, can be traced near the River Glenderamackin. In the village itself the church dates only from 1777 and the pubs are older: the Horse and Farrier has the date 1688 over the door and was the place where Wordsworth and De Quincey took afternoon tea every Tuesday when Wordsworth was making regular trips from Grasmere to Penrith on postal business.

Torver, a hamlet south of Coniston at the junction of the roads to Broughton and Ulverston, has access to a pleasant walk along the shore of Coniston Water and also, from Torver High Common, one of the best overall views of the Coniston fells, with Dow Crag and the Old Man of Coniston to the forefront. There is a profusion of cairns, possible stone circles and other prehistoric earthworks on Torver High Common and the adjacent Little Arrow Moor.

Troutbeck is one of the show villages of the Lake District, with well over a dozen seventeenth- and early eighteenth-century statesman farmhouses. The village straggles for over a mile along a shelf above the Trout Beck valley, with clusters of dwellings around a number of wells from which communal water supplies were obtained. These clusters are connected by a bewildering array of lanes, tracks and paths, re-emphasising the scattered nature of the village. The focus of attention for most people is the National Trust property at Town End, the farmhouse of the Browne family from the time it was built in 1623 until it came into the care of the NT some 320 years later. A classic example of a statesman farmhouse, with a marvellously authentic interior, Town End should be on every itinerary, both for its architectural style, with cylindrical chimneys, slate roof, mullioned windows, and (around the back) a spinning gallery, and for the details of its interior, with cheese press, mangle and wooden washing machine amongst the exhibits.

Ullswater is a particularly attractive lake because of the variety of scenery encompassed in its twisting course from the head of the lake in the mountains near Patterdale to the sylvan beauty of the lower reaches around Pooley Bridge. Incomparably the best way to see it is by steamer along the length of the lake from Glenridding Pier to Pooley Bridge, with an intermediate stop at Howtown on the east shore. The main road along the west shore has a number of parking places and passes Gowbarrow Park (with the waterfall of Aira Force near at hand) and Glencoyne, but motorists are better served by the narrow road along the east shore, passing several secluded bays thick with sailing craft in summer on the way to Howtown and Martindale. An easy walk from Martindale new church leads to the top of Hallin Fell, from where there is an excellent view of the lake. Walkers will be particularly keen to try the lakeside path from Patterdale below Place Fell to Howtown, often touted as the most picturesque low-level walk in the Lake District.

Ulverston is a market town close to the southern boundary of the National Park which has seen better days but is nevertheless well worth seeing. The better days were at their height in the early nineteenth century, when iron ore, slate and locally manufactured goods were being exported direct from Ulverston, then linked to the sea by a short canal. The canal has silted up, largely because Barrow-in-Furness usurped Ulverston's role as a port, and now the town relies on its function as a market centre together with some tourist trade and a little manufacturing. Worth a visit are Hoad Hill, where the lighthouse is a memorial to Sir John Barrow, a son of Ulverston who was Under-Secretary to the Admiralty for forty years, and the remains of the canal, including the basin, Brow Bridge lock and the pier at Canal Foot.

Wasdale Head has a spectacularly beautiful location, surrounded by some of the highest and best peaks in the Lake District and close to the shores of Wastwater, with the forbidding wall of the Wastwater Screes on the far side of the lake. The Norse were the first to settle here, taking on the backbreaking task of clearing the flat valley floor of the boulders brought down by all the winter torrents of preceding centuries. The fruits of their labours are the present valley pastures, divided by astonishingly thick walls containing all those boulders. Heaps of stones can also be found in the fields where there were just too many to put in the walls. The tiny church, with its bellcote and combined nave and chancel, dates from the early eighteenth century. The hamlet, and in particular the Wasdale Head Inn, was mecca for early British rock climbing enthusiasts; now the inn caters generally for less energetic tourists.

Wastwater is the deepest of the lakes, with its deepest parts below sea level, and it is also one of the most austere, with the forbidding wall of the Wastwater Screes along much of the southern shore and rocky margins around the remainder, so that there is a very limited fish population – just trout and char. The compensation, however, is a series of stunning views up the lake to the mountains around Wasdale Head: Yewbarrow, Kirk Fell, Great Gable, Lingmell, Scafell Pike and Scafell. There are delightful hamlets at each end of the lake – Wasdale Head below the mountains, with the track up the dale to Sty Head very obvious on the lower slopes of Great Gable, and Nether Wasdale (Strands) below the foot of the lake.

Watendlath is a delectable though sometimes too crowded hamlet at the end of a very narrow road which leaves Borrowdale in the woods at Ashness Gate, crosses Ashness Bridge – probably *the* most photographed bridge in the Lake District, with Derwentwater and Skiddaw as a splendid background – and passes another good viewpoint for Derwentwater, the so-called Surprise View, before reaching the cluster of farmhouses and the shallow bowl containing Watendlath Tarn. The surroundings are delectable and there is added literary interest, since one of the farmhouses was supposedly the heroine's home in Hugh Walpole's *Judith Paris*, yet commercialism has commendably been kept at bay, though there is a pleasant tea garden. The best way to reach Watendlath, avoiding all the problems of too many cars on the too-narrow road, is to walk over Grange Fell from Rosthwaite; another bonus of this walk is the sudden bird's-eye view of tarn and hamlet from near the highest point of the walk.

Windermere lake caters admirably for the more gregarious Lake District visitor; the seeker after solitude will have to travel further west to find a lake to suit. The town is similarly brash and vulgar by local standards, with nothing of great historical interest and a rash of gift shops near the station. The attractions of the lake nevertheless go deeper than the steamers and pleasure craft which throng its relatively calm waters. It is the longest lake and as a result is a lake of many moods, with quiet bays and wooded islands adding to its beauty. The lake occupies two basins scooped out by the glaciers, with a shallower middle section around Belle Isle. Amongst the attractions around the shores of the lake are Fell Foot country park at its southern tip, the promenade at Bowness, the National Park visitor centre at Brockhole, the boat landings at Waterhead, the site of the Roman fort of Galava near Ambleside at the head of the lake, and, on the western shore, Wray Castle, the wooded Claife Heights, the ferry crossing from Far Sawrey back to Bowness, and the steamer pier and steam railway at Lakeside.

Winster is a hamlet at the head of the beautiful Winster valley, which runs parallel to and east of Windermere. The old post office in the hamlet, a diminutive early seventeenth-century cottage, is famous and highly photogenic. Beyond Bowland Bridge the river flows between Cartmel Fell and the slopes of Whitbarrow Scar, a nature reserve with a good deal of exposed limestone pavement and a distinctive flora, before passing close to Witherslack on its way to Morecambe Bay. To the east of Whitbarrow Scar is the Lyth Valley, famous for its damson blossom in May and hence for its damson jam and wine.

Wray Castle, close to the north-western shores of Windermere and only 5km (3 miles) from Ambleside, sometimes deceives the unwary with its medieval appearance, but in reality it is an extravagant Victorian pile constructed to the order of James Dawson, a Liverpool doctor, in the 1840s. It is set in attractively wooded grounds, with a lake frontage and paths leading to Claife Heights and Far Sawrey. The National Nature Reserve at Blelham Tarn is nearby.

Yanwath, very close to the motorway, is a hamlet near Penrith with one building of real distinction, Yanwath Hall. John de Sutton erected a pele tower here in 1323, and this heavy-looking defensive structure survives as part of the present building, together with the hall, kitchen and courtyard added in the fifteenth century. The pele is a fine example of the characteristic Cumbrian defensive tower, with a tunnel-vaulted ground floor, mullioned and transomed first floor windows, and sandstone battlements with little corner turrets capping the whole structure.

INDEX

Page numbers in *italics* indicate illustrations